I0137409

ONE CONGREGATION'S
JOURNEY *of* CHANGE

A GUIDE TO ENRICHING RELATIONSHIPS IN YOUR CONGREGATION

DR. TUSSY SHNIDER

No part of this publication may be reproduced in whole or in part, or stored in a retrieval system, or transmitted in any form or by any means, electronic, mechanical, photocopying, recording, or otherwise, without written permission of the author, except for the inclusion of brief quotations in a review. For information regarding permission, please write to:
info@barringerpublishing.com

Copyright © 2019 Dr. Tussy Shnider
All rights reserved.

Barringer Publishing, Naples, Florida
www.barringerpublishing.com
Cover, graphics, layout design by Linda Duider

ISBN: 978-0-9989069-9-7

Library of Congress Cataloging-in-Publication Data
Journey of Change / A Guide To Enriching Relationships In Your Congregation

Printed in U.S.A.

ONE FAMILY at TEMPLE SHALOM

Relational Judaism, implemented as One Family at Temple Shalom, is a way of thinking, a way of doing things. It is who we strive to be. At Temple Shalom, we are in the midst of a transformation—a culture shift, from programmatical/ transactional thinking, attitudes, and behavior to a culture based on the relationship of one member to another, of member to Temple, and of member to Torah and God. Believing in the value and sacredness of relationships, many aspects of life at Temple Shalom continue to be impacted. From the first contact of a newcomer to Temple Shalom through the years of being a part of our Temple family, the experience of belonging is much more than a transaction of paying dues and "purchasing" the rights of membership. Everyone who wishes to be a part of our Temple family determines their own annual pledge which we call L'Shalom. This pledge system and the discontinuation of the building fund have removed financial barriers to membership and participation in our One Family. Our ultimate goal is to build a community of engaged congregants, a religious home in which the connection between Temple and congregant is centered on our members' needs and what is important to them. Creating the systems that promote relationships and an environment that is conducive to connecting with others are our tools for furthering this transformation.

Inspired by the Temple Shalom Website

CONTENTS

FOREWORD

A few years ago, a presentation from Dr. Ron Wolfson led to a shocking revelation: we've been looking at congregations from the wrong perspective. After years of using a transactional model—touting programs to attract members and evaluating success based on head counts—we lost the essence of a congregation as a place where people came to establish sacred relationships. The stories he shared of individuals feeling disconnected in their congregations resonated with comments I heard from our membership. Particularly familiar was the story of a woman who resigned despite weekly Shabbat service attendance. She explained to her rabbi, "Rabbi, I know you, and you know me. But after fifteen years, I don't know anyone else, and they don't know me."

This relational revelation struck home for me. Belonging to a synagogue or a congregation of any faith should provide a sense of *kehillah kedosha,* or holy community, while strengthening one's religious identity and a sense of purpose. We cannot accomplish such a goal without prioritizing value-based relationships. To shift our priorities, I knew that I needed partners from within the leadership and membership of the congregation. Like Moses, who learned from Jethro to establish a team, I returned home to Temple Shalom and began to share this new concept with our staff and our lay leadership. An assessment with key constituents and leadership confirmed that we were indeed stuck in the transactional model and needed to change our direction. Primed for this new endeavor, we assembled a team led primarily by Dr. Tussy Shnider and her husband Neil to kick-off this exciting new concept in our congregation. One Family, as we branded the initiative, began with a successful opening event, where the sanctuary overflowed with individuals eager to embrace this new concept.

The transformation rapidly progressed, with dozens volunteering their time and talents in task forces exploring how One Family could shape the future of our congregation. This initiative, evolving from those initial groups, is now part of our identity as a congregation. Over the course of only a few years, we have seen several impactful changes: an emphasis for individuals to engage with other participants at programs and worship services; on-going relationship building efforts through informal programming; the creation of a staff position dedicated to member engagement; and the switch from a dues-based membership to a voluntary pledge system.

I am grateful to Tussy for her indispensable leadership, and especially for writing *One Congregation's Journey of Change: A Guide to Enriching Relationships in Your Congregation*. This book provides experience and guidelines that will enable other synagogues, as well as faith communities from across the religious spectrum, to establish value-based relationships within their congregations. Every house of worship has the potential to create spiritually meaningful relationships with fellow individuals, clergy, and the Divine.

May Dr. Shnider's book inspire you all to create your own One Family, with many connections for all who enter.

> With Blessings for Peace,
> Rabbi Adam F. Miller

INTRODUCTION

BACKGROUND

I first learned about the concept of a relationship-based congregation in the mid-1990s when I attended a presentation at a biennial meeting of the Northeast Lakes Region of the Union for Reform Judaism (URJ). The presenters were from a congregation in our region that had been selected to be a pilot congregation to implement the concept as described by Rabbi Richard Address, a Union for Reform Judaism leader known for his work regarding Jewish family concerns, especially "sacred aging." Rabbi Address had written his doctoral thesis on the sacredness of relationships. He stated:

> Everything from architecture to grand-parenting is in flux and change. Yet, it seems that one issue of life remains constant. Relationships. I am a believer in what I have come to call the "theology of relationships." This is not very high brow. It is pretty simple, actually. It is a belief that the most powerful aspect of our lives, especially as we age, are the relationships that we have. The desire to be with other people, to share life in all of its aspects, is a key to health of the soul and thus attitudes of living … relationships are primary and the nurturing of these relationships is a key to health and fulfillment.[1]

Rabbi Address had envisioned congregations that functioned based on that value—the sacredness of relationships. Several congregations around the country had been invited to implement the concept. Each of their approaches differed from the others. He described these congregations based in relationships as "caring communities."

As the presenters at that mid-1990s biennial described what their congregation was doing, I became more and more captivated by their depiction of the experience created for their members. They referred to their process as creating

---

a Caring Community, and this name became associated with their congregation. The thought that kept going through my mind was *That's what it should be like to be a member of a temple!* A few years later, when working toward my MSW degree, I was fortunate to learn more about their Caring Community Congregation when I was doing an internship at another Midwestern congregation. One of my responsibilities was to introduce the relationship-based congregation concept to the board of this congregation. Working with the internship congregation's Rabbi and their president, I provided materials and explanations, arranged for the Rabbi and me to visit the Caring Community Congregation and arranged for the Cantor of the Caring Community congregation (the staff person for their Caring Community) to visit us and speak to our Board. The more I learned about the concept, the more I believed in its value.

Fast forward thirteen years to the fall of 2013. My husband, Neil, and I had moved to a warmer climate and joined Temple Shalom in Naples, Florida, an already wonderful congregation. In the early months of our membership in this congregation, I became aware of the many interesting activities developed by this congregation. The Religious School, award-winning preschool, adult education classes, social justice/social action programs, and so much more were all available and, from what I could see, well done. The leaders were accessible and communication with the congregation was good. Members of the congregation seemed happy, and proud of the congregation's fifty-year history.

After attending a program focused on the development of relationships by sharing stories, I gave our Rabbi, Adam Miller, a one-sheet explanation of Rabbi Address' concept of relationship-based congregations that I had prepared for my internship congregation. Not long after, Rabbi Miller gave Neil and me copies of Dr. Ron Wolfson's book, *Relational Judaism: Using the Power of Relationships to Transform the Jewish Community* (Jewish Lights Publishing). He asked us both to read the book. We did, and we were both very intrigued. Shortly after that, much to my amazement, Rabbi Miller asked the two of us to chair the Relational Judaism Initiative that would later become known in our congregation as One Family. About a year and a half later, with my husband serving as President of the congregation, I found the need for an additional partner in leading our Initiative. I asked a long-time leader of the congregation (Past President, current Board Member, Membership Chair and Caring Committee Chair) to work as a third Co-Chair with Neil and me. She accepted, and we have been working together ever since. Her knowledge of the congregation, long-time members and new members, has been a valuable asset to our partnership.

My book was written as a description of two values-based changes from a transactional/programmatically based culture to a relationship-based culture. A transactional/programmatical culture refers to a focus on the programs offered by a congregation—religious school, preschool, bar/bat mitzvah preparation, adult education, etc. It is saying, "We offer these programs and services. Come and join us." In many respects, it is an outreach process seeking to bring in new members. A relational culture reflects a focus on the relationships of one member to another, of the member to the organization, and of the member to Torah (Bible) and to God. It is a way of thinking that impacts the way things are done and the way decisions are made. Relational thinking is an inreach process that is focused on the current members, enriching their experience by the enhancing their development of relationships. The two relationships to which our Temple Shalom process has been devoted and about which this book is written are the member-to-member relationships and the member-to-congregation relationships. The beginnings of our process focused on the member-to-member relationship component and the projects we implemented toward the enrichment of those relationships. The member-to-congregation component is found in the transition from a system of annual standard commitment (a traditional dues system) to a voluntary pledge system. There is overlap and blurring of the two types of relationships (e.g., when relationships among members are strengthened, so is the relationship of the member to the organization). Both kinds of relationships are basic to our relationship with God. The importance of our relationships with each other and with God applies to all faiths.

This book was written as a step-by-step guide for congregation leaders who are looking for a meaningful way to inspire a new direction and a shift in thinking that focuses on values, which can lead to a congregational transformation. While an increase in membership numbers may result from this congregational transformation, that is not necessarily a primary goal. This book was written in the spirit of the Union for Reform Judaism and the Women of Reform Judaism where we were taught to share our experiences, especially our successes, with other congregations.

This book was written in the first person because that is how I experienced the process. It does not in any way imply that I, alone, led or am responsible for any success had by our Initiative. Nothing could be further from the truth! Our process has been a group process in every way, involving as many members as possible, drawing in leaders and participants at every turn.

This kind of congregational transformation involves building on the structure that is already in place, continuing that which is working well, expanding and adjusting where needed. It requires flexibility and an open mind—a willingness to consider and accept new ideas and to listen, listen, listen. It requires leaders that are willing to share territory and welcome additional leaders. And every member of the congregation becomes an ambassador to the larger community.

Every congregation's challenges, needs, strengths, and opportunities will be different, resulting in different expressions of the concept. But once the congregation leadership grasps the concept and understands its value, there are unlimited ways to create a "One Family" in your congregation.

Organization of This Book

The transformational process alone cannot be expected to "cure" a dysfunctional organization. The more effective the congregation is as an organization, the greater the chance for success of the transformation process. **Chapter One** identifies some basic, best practices of an effective organization and provides a checklist to aid in evaluating the readiness of your congregation for a change process.

For most Reform Jewish congregations, becoming a relationship-based congregation involves a congregational culture shift, a transformation from transactional thinking, attitudes, and behavior to a culture based on the relationship of one member to another, of the member to the Temple, and of the member to Torah and God. Chapters Two, Three, and Four are focused on the principles and implementation of Relational Judaism as we interpreted it in our One Family Initiative. Our One Family Initiative addresses all the relationships listed above by **emphasizing the member-to-member relationship** and the **member-to-congregation relationship**.

Getting started can be a daunting step in the transformation process. While this will vary from congregation to congregation, putting together a team of creative and enthusiastic people will provide a valuable source for brainstorming and developing ideas. Our beginning is described in **Chapter Two**. Hopefully, reading about our beginning will reduce the stress of getting started in your congregation.

This transformation process does not require disrupting the congregation's organizational structure. Working within the existing structure and with the people already in place, we developed another set of systems and projects designed to provide opportunities for connection and engagement. In our process, we worked in cooperation with many existing committees, projects, and affiliate groups that were in place and functioning well including, but not limited to, the Caring Committee, Shabbat Greeters, Building and Grounds Committee, Ushers Committee, Membership Committee, Sisterhood, Men's Club, Mitzvah Day, and, of course, the Temple Board. Our focus was the creation of opportunities to connect and engage. New programs that formed were "bottom up" in nature, emerging from the needs and interests expressed by members. The difference between the systems to which I am referring and the traditional idea of programs will become clearer as you read about them in **Chapter Three**.

Regarding the projects described in Chapter Three, please keep in mind that the projects we implemented are ones that emerged from our process of brainstorming and trial and error. They may or may not work for your congregation. Attempting to copy each of our projects is not a guarantee of success. **It is my hope that <u>our process</u> will be helpful as a guide to getting started and the description of our projects will help to clarify the kinds of opportunities you can provide to move your process forward.**

As our process developed, we also learned about Audacious Hospitality as presented by Rabbi Rick Jacobs, President of The Union for Reform Judaism. The similarities between Audacious Hospitality and Relational Judaism became clear to us. These connections are discussed in **Chapter Four**.

As we worked together, we became more aware of the core values of Reform Judaism—loving kindness, respect, and *tikkun olam* (repairing the world), and the expressions of those values—inclusion, diversity, welcoming, connectedness, engagement, and the importance of relationships. We also realized we had to reflect these values in every way we functioned as an organization. It became clear that we had to remove the barriers to membership and participation in Temple life, to make it easier for the Jews of our community to express their Jewish selves. In **Chapter Five**, the values discussion continues with the focus on the financial support from our Temple members. This chapter introduces the shift from a traditional annual commitment system (frequently called dues and hereafter referred to as dues) to a **voluntary pledge system, altering the relationship of members to the temple**. This journey is presented from the beginning—from researching the concept, to planning the change, to the introduction of the plan to the congregation, to the implementation of the new system, and to the early results of our change.

A transformational change process in an organization involves communication with the membership. For the first two and a half years, much of this communication was done by the leaders and members of the One Family Team, by the Rabbi, and by Temple Board members. Some of these responsibilities shifted to our new Marketing and Communications Committee in the summer of 2016. The marketing of the One Family concepts and activities is presented in **Chapter Six**.

Various means of evaluating the progress of change are presented in **Chapter Seven**. Measurement of change in the congregational setting can be challenging, but some objective measures can be used.

Chapter Eight summarizes our process and looks to the future.

Some of the chapters have appendices providing samples of the materials we developed and used. These are presented here as further explanation and additional aids for use by other congregations attempting a relational congregation change.

Additional Thoughts

Dealing with Resistance—It is also likely that you will meet with some resistance to change. Inertia is a powerful force. For some individuals, any change creates discomfort. Others will provide various reasons for their desire to keep things the way they "have always been." Some may not even know the real reasons they would prefer to keep things as they are. The following are some frequently given (sometimes unspoken) reasons:

- Fear of the unknown

- Habit—comfort with the current ways things are done

- Fear of losing power and authority

- Fear of being displaced or replaced

- Territorial attitudes

- Concern about "more work"

- Concern about costs

With sensitivity, these concerns can be overcome. Some suggestions for dealing with resistance include:

- **Gaining the support of the leadership, both professional and lay**, is a must. The endorsements of the rabbi(s), the cantor, the administrator, and the president are essential and best done before introducing Relational Judaism to the rest of the leaders. The support of the other officers, members of the board, and other congregational leaders and influential members will be more likely to create a positive outcome and will go a long way to facilitate acceptance of change. In our case, it was the Rabbi and the President who had the vision that Relational Judaism would be a meaningful direction for our congregation. They were the ones who introduced the concept of Relational Judaism to the congregation leadership and have continued to be supportive throughout our implementation process (as have the presidents that followed). This process is described in Chapter Two.

- **Educating the members of the congregation and providing information about the progress of the changes** can reduce the uncertainty that underlies resistance. Frequent bulletin articles, positive comments from the *bimah* (raised platform at the front of the sanctuary where the service is lead) by both the rabbi and congregation leaders, and frequent references at events to the change process by name will help create the sense that the whole congregation is included and involved and moving in the same direction. More information regarding education and marketing is provided in Chapter Six.

- **Involvement of as many people as possible** will give many members of the congregation a sense of having input, a sense of empowerment that can reduce resistance. Delegating responsibilities and creating work groups are a means of creating involvement. And it is a Jewish way of leading! More about the value of empowerment and leading Jewishly in Chapter One.

- **If needed, have one-on-one chats with those that continue to resist**. Listen with sensitivity, allowing them to voice their concerns. Try to find common ground and comfortable ways for them to get involved.

To Readers Who Are Not Jewish—If you are involved in a church, you may say, "That's what we do already. What's the big deal?" In fact, I hope some of what you read here feels familiar. The truth is that some of these ideas are borrowed from the behaviors found in churches. However, you may also be searching for meaningful ways to increase the relational nature of your congregation, for ways to focus on your values. Indeed, much of my review of the professional literature was based on church research. But just as I found meaningful data in the church research, I believe you can find valuable information in this synagogue-based experience. I hope you will read on and, of greater importance, I hope you will find some concepts and activities that will be helpful to your congregation. For your convenience, a glossary of the Hebrew terms I used can be found at the back of the book.

Be Patient—Cultural change in a congregation does not happen overnight. There is nothing fast about it. It is a slow and ongoing process. It is best not to attempt too many new projects simultaneously. When multiple ideas are being considered, prioritize them based on which ones are doable, which ones will make an impact, and which ones have passionate advocates. Begin with three or four, adding one or two more at a time as passionate leaders emerge. It may take several years to see—and feel—real change. There will likely be some projects that do not work, some that work for a while with interest waning over time, and hopefully some real successes. You will need to evaluate your process and your projects as you go. You and your co-workers must make decisions regarding dropping a project or adjusting and continuing a project.

A Caveat—There are many ways to achieve the goal of a relational transformation. Our experience is only one way to get from here to there. I do not believe that our way is the only way and I do not profess to know the best way for all congregations. The information is presented here in the spirit of helpfulness in hopes that you and your congregation will not find it too daunting to undertake a value-based relational transformation initiative or to change from a dues system to a voluntary pledge system. I have presented our successes and our flops—our lemons and our lemonade! What did not work for us might work for you. And I hope your team will come up with additional ideas.

THANK YOU

I thank Rabbi Richie Address for introducing congregation leaders to the importance and sacredness of relationships. This concept is so basic to all that we do in congregation life. Thank you to Dr. Ron Wolfson (Fingerhut Professor of Education at American Jewish University) whose book was the motivation for the One Family Initiative at Temple Shalom. I thank Rabbi Adam Miller and then Temple Shalom President Yale Freeman for their vision and for the opportunity for Neil and me to be a part of this Relational Judaism experience at Temple Shalom. I thank them for their support throughout our process. I thank the leaders and staff, lay and professional, of Temple Shalom for their trust and their support. Thank you to the members of the One Family Team who put time and effort into the One Family projects. Thank you to the generous members who stepped forward to provide the funds needed to make the projects happen. Thank you to all the members of the congregation who participated (and continue to participate) in the One Family projects and in any project or program associated with Temple Shalom; you are the heart and soul of Relational Judaism at Temple Shalom. And a special thank you to my co-chairs, my partners, Bobbie Katz and my husband, Neil Shnider, who made this journey a joy.

* * * *

If your congregation engages in a Relational Judaism initiative of transformation, I would love feedback at various stages in your process. I would love to know what worked and what didn't work for you, any significant moments and responses from members of your congregation, etc. If you have questions, contact me at drtussyshnider@gmail.com.

B'Shalom,
D. Tussy Shnider, Ph.D.

CHAPTER ONE

BEST PRACTICES – CONGREGATIONS AS ORGANIZATIONS

> You stand this day, all of you, before the Lord your God—your tribal heads, your elders, and your officials, all the men of Israel, your children, your wives, even the stranger within your camp, from woodchopper to waterdrawer—to enter into the covenant of the Lord your God, which the Lord your God is concluding with you this day, with its sanctions; to the end that He may establish you this day as his people and be your God, as He promised you and as he swore to your fathers, Abraham, Isaac, and Jacob. I make this covenant with its sanctions, not with you alone, but both with those who are standing here with us this day before the Lord our God and with those who are not with us here this day.[1]
>
> Deuteronomy: 29: 9-14, translation from TANAKH

Becoming a relationship-based organization is not likely to transform a dysfunctional congregation into a functional one. If the basic operations of the organization do not effectively move the congregation toward the achievement of the stated goals, provide the services expected by the members, and reflect the values expected of a religious institution, no amount of effort to create relationships will magically transform the congregation into an organization that functions well. Some basic organizational principles are understood by management mavens to create effective organizations; some of these principles have been shown empirically to apply to religious congregations.[2] Knowledge of these principles, theoretical and empirical, and a sincere effort to implement them as standard practice in a congregation will provide a foundation for the experience of transforming a transactional, program-based congregation into a value-based relational one. Just as a foundation was laid for Torah to be declared valid for all generations (see quote at the beginning of this chapter), your congregation will do well to assess where you are in regards to organizational best practices. A firm foundation will enhance the outcome of your efforts. Some basic information regarding these principles is presented here with the suggestion for organizational self-evaluation regarding these principles before embarking on a journey of cultural change. A readiness checklist is provided in Appendix 1A (pp. 89-95).

CONGREGATIONS AS MEMBERSHIP ORGANIZATIONS

An organization is defined as "a consciously coordinated social unit composed of two or more people that functions on a relatively continuous basis to achieve a common goal or set of goals."[3] Anthony and Young divide organizations into two major groups, for use in for-profit and nonprofit organizations. They define the functioning of for-profit organizations as "decisions made by management are intended to increase (or at least maintain) profits. Success is measured, to a significant degree, by the amount of profit the organization earns." They define the nonprofit organization as "an organization whose goal as something other than earning a profit for its owners. Usually, the goal is to provide services."[4] Peter Drucker, often characterized as the management guru, describes nonprofit organizations as follows:

> "The 'non-profit' institution neither supplies goods or services nor controls. Its 'product' is neither a pair of shoes nor an effective regulation. **Its product is a changed human being. The non-profit institutions are human-change agents** [emphasis added]. Their 'product' is a cured patient, a child that learns, a young man or woman grown into a self-respecting adult; a changed human life altogether."[5]

Synagogues and churches are among these human change agents, providing their members with opportunities for spiritual, educational, and social growth and providing their communities with needed social services.

A further division of nonprofit organizations, as described by Anthony and Young, is by sectors based on their principal focus; healthcare organizations, educational organizations, human service and arts organizations, government organizations, and member organizations. They define member organizations as "those whose purpose is to render services to their members."[6] They include religious organizations (such as churches and synagogues) in this member organization group by virtue of the way in which they are structured and governed. Unlike the "traditional" model of governance in which an organization's guardians (leaders) provide services to consumers or beneficiaries, in the membership model "the beneficiaries are not 'third parties' identified as having a social need, but the 'guardians' themselves."[7]

As membership organizations, congregations are usually dependent on their members for financial and human resources. This is certainly true of most Reform Jewish congregations. As a human resource, the members volunteer to provide a large part of the work that takes place in congregation life. Most congregations function with a small paid staff, the number of employees determined by the congregation's size, needs, and finances. The members govern, chair and serve on committees, lead and participate in programs, and generally function as unpaid staff. As financial resources, members function in two ways—providing income to the congregation in their annual commitment (for synagogues, usually in the form of dues) and acting as fund-raisers, developing and staffing projects designed to bring in additional monies. While some synagogues have their own foundations, well-funded by endowments contributing substantially to their budgets, most rely heavily or totally on dues income from members. Congregations sometimes apply for and receive grants from outside foundations. Reform Jewish congregations do not receive funds from a centralized organizational structure. Quite the opposite is the case. They pay an annual commitment to the umbrella organization, the Union for Reform Judaism (URJ), to be affiliates. Therefore, the monies necessary to support the staff, building, programs, and affiliations of the organization must come from member dues or other fund-raising efforts done by the members.

Thus, the members are the most important resource for the congregation in the volunteer leadership and services they provide, the dues they pay (or other financial support system), and the funds they raise. The very survival of the congregation depends on the commitment of the members in time, effort, and dollars. If Reform Jewish congregations are to continue to exist, providing the means to educate each generation insuring Judaism's future, the members of the congregation must believe in the synagogue's ability to deliver services. And the members must be committed enough to give of their time and their money.

What happens to that commitment when a congregation's effectiveness is diminished? It is likely that, over time, a discontented membership will be reluctant to provide the money and effort that the congregation needs to exist. Some members may leave the congregation. When this situation arises, the leaders may look for ways to improve the congregation's effectiveness and may want to identify the factors in management that have been demonstrated to be associated with more effective functioning.

CONGREGATIONS AS EFFECTIVE ORGANIZATIONS

Organizational Effectiveness

What does one mean by "organizational effectiveness?" How would such a concept be measured? Unlike for-profit organizations that describe success with the objective measure of the bottom line (i.e., did the organization make or increase profit in a specified period?), the measurement of effectiveness in the non-profit world, especially congregations, can be murky. Various approaches for such measurement in non-profit organizations have been suggested, including measuring the extent to which the organization is meeting its goals or measuring the relationship of inputs and outputs. Such measurements are not readily applied to religious congregations. As stated by Anthony and Young, "Religious organizations have a particularly difficult problem in deciding on the programs to be undertaken and in measuring the value of services rendered. ('Souls saved per pew hour preached' is not a feasible measurement!)"[8] As stated by Shnider,

> Even though religious congregations seek to make changes in the way their members feel and behave, in what they know, to influence the quality of their lives, and to constructively impact their communities, congregations have no way of quantifying their performance regarding these changes. Because there

was no entrance evaluation administered when a person or family joins the congregation, there is no baseline with which to compare. Further, it is difficult to objectively measure changes in such subjective concepts as a congregant's sense of self-actualization, sense of community, understanding of Jewish [Christian] theological perspectives, status, or quality of relationships with others.[9]

One approach to determining organizational effectiveness does, however, provide a basis for measurably (quantitatively) describing a congregation's effectiveness. This approach, as suggested by Forbes, is *reputational effectiveness*, defined as "effectiveness according to the self-reported opinions of some set of persons, usually clients, staff, or outside professionals who are familiar with the organization at hand."[10] Herman and Renz, describe this perspective as a concept that "considers reality or some parts of reality to be created by the beliefs, knowledge, and actions of the people."[11] Stated another way, *"effectiveness is judgement."*[12] I used this concept in developing measurement scales for Reform Jewish congregations, explaining "The recognition of the subjective nature of the evaluations does not reduce the credibility of the evaluations; rather it establishes the importance of the subjectivity of those evaluations."[13]

Some Factors Associated with Congregational Effectiveness

Many factors contribute to the "effectiveness" of a non-profit organization. Volumes have been written on the subject. It would require a book with a different focus to fully address the best management practices associated with non-profit organizations even when limiting the subject to religious congregations. However, frequently appearing in the literature are several factors that have been shown empirically and repeatedly to influence organizational effectiveness. **These factors include (but are not limited to) shared vision, board development, self-evaluation, and member empowerment.** By no means are these presented here as a comprehensive set of factors associated with effectiveness, but rather as some behaviors that, congregationally speaking, have been demonstrated to significantly contribute to their reputational effectiveness.

Shared Vision refers to factors in the organization's management that demonstrate a broad group process of thought and action regarding the reason for the organization's existence and the organization's future.[14] This construct includes the process by which the organization's values, mission, goals, and strategies are identified and the transmission of this information to the organization's members. There is a substantial body of evidence that clarity of mission and goals, representing shared vision and values, that are determined in an inclusive process and used in decision-making and to evaluate progress toward goals, contributes to organizational effectiveness.[15] Specifically, shared vision has been shown to be significantly and positively correlated with reputational effectiveness for members of Reform Jewish congregations. The higher the reported level of shared vision, the higher the perceived level of reputational effectiveness. It appears that, for the members of these congregations, **a sense of knowing the congregation's mission and goals is associated with more favorable feelings regarding the congregation's effectiveness.**[16]

Board Development refers to factors in the organization's management that demonstrate a desire to educate board members regarding the organization and regarding the role of the board and its members as it relates to the management of the organization.[17] This construct includes practices designed to provide board members with information regarding the organization's history and its place in its community, the board's responsibilities to the organization, and individual responsibilities as board members.[18] Board development has been another focus of attention among researchers of nonprofit organization effectiveness. Concern centers on the apparent lack of understanding among board members regarding their role and the lack of board training and education. One dismal description of boards is stated by Gibelman, Gelman, and Pollack: "We suggest that many nonprofits totter on the brink of serious problems, if not disaster."[19] Included in their list of symptoms of these boards are "board members who are unprepared for meetings and who fail to keep abreast of organizational developments" and "lack of clarification of the respective roles of board and staff."[20]

Other researchers found strong associations between board development opportunities and effective board functioning and satisfaction with the board experience. In my research specifically with Reform Jewish congregations, I found that opportunities for board education were significantly and positively associated with reputational effectiveness.[21] **The higher the reported level of board development that was reported, the higher the rating of reputational**

effectiveness. Gibelman, Gelman, and Pollack summarized the case for systematic and ongoing board training as being

> ... essential to knowledgeable governance. Elements of an effective board development program include orienting new and continuing board members on an annual basis, providing continuing education in policy making, and promoting continuous opportunities for the board to assess its own performance and that of the organization.[22]

Self-evaluation refers to factors in the organization's management that demonstrate a desire to understand the positive and negative results of board decisions and congregation programs through self-examination. This construct includes efforts to review the board's performance and the performance of the programs and projects that the board develops. In the Holland, Leslie, and Holzhalb study of the culture and patterns of twenty-two more effective and less effective boards, they describe the patterns of more effective boards regarding the evaluation of performance:

> A significant distinction was that the more effective boards directed attention to their **processes** [emphasis added] for dealing with issues as well as the substance. After struggling with difficult problems and coming to conclusions, these boards often took some time to reflect together on what they could learn from how they had dealt with issues, what assumptions had guided those efforts, and what might be done differently to improve their future efforts.[23]

In the same study, patterns of less-effective boards were described as follows:

> [Less effective] boards seldom raised questions about their own performance or did so only under the duress of some crisis in the organization, such as declining income, public embarrassment, substantial loss of market share, or the need

to replace the CEO. At such times, board members found themselves struggling with diverse individual interests, competing demands from coalitions of members, challenges from constituency representatives, or threats to public credibility and support. Typical attempts to contain the disruption included finding the least stressful of familiar solutions and searching for answers within the accepted framework of assumptions and practices. Often the result was blaming some individual (a member of the staff or board) for failure and expecting that finding an acceptable replacement for him or her would solve the problem.[24]

A review of the organizational literature revealed a consistent significant positive correlation between self-evaluation and reputational effectiveness. (However, in my research, the self-evaluation factor was presented only to a small sample of congregation leaders resulting in an unclear relationship between the two variables. It is possible that the relationship between self-evaluation and effectiveness would be clearer with a larger sample.)

Member Empowerment refers to factors in the organization's management that promote the ability of the membership to participate in the life and leadership of the organization. This construct includes those aspects of organization life that provide members with a sense of ownership, the inclusion of members and their ideas in programs and decision making, the accessibility of the organization's leaders to the members, the ease with which members can be involved and move into leadership positions, and the sense of being valued that is held by members of the organization.

It is the use of power and the balance of power that is often the cause for concern in organizations. Harris writes of the tension resulting from the lack of clarity regarding the power of boards. She attributes these tensions to organizational history, the interdependence of board and staff and the multiplicity of constituencies. She further describes the variations of the power relationships based on the model of governance of the organization—traditional, membership, or entrepreneurial. Congregations, being membership organizations, have a "closed circle" linkage between the organization's guardians (those with positive concern for the organizations long-term survival) and the organization's beneficiaries (those served by the organization).[25] In the membership model, the beneficiaries are the guardians themselves. Harris describes the power struggle between board and staff in this model stating the professional staff "may resent the threat to their ability to exercise professional judgments which is implicit in a situation in which 'clients' are also employers and managers."[26]

Several researchers addressed the power factor by studying the flow of information. Leduc and Block make the connection between power and the ability to control the flow of organizational information. "Intentionally or unintentionally, the executive director can influence the policy decision capability of the board by either stressing or withholding certain information."[27] Pfeffer writes:

> . . . information and the certainty it can provide, is a source of power. There is little doubt that it can be used as part of a very important political strategy — getting one's way through analysis. . .[This] means that those in control of the facts and the analysis can exercise substantial influence.[28]
>
> Given the availability of multiple bases for making a decision, one strategic use of power and influence involves advocating the employment of standards that favor one's own position.[29]
>
> Of course, employing information selectively means strategically ignoring information that does not advance one's own point of view.[30]

Centralization and decentralization of power is another mechanism discussed by researchers. McGaw, in his quantitative and qualitative study of congregational commitment, compared a more liberal, mainline Presbyterian congregation with a more conservative, charismatic Presbyterian congregation. McGaw describes the mainline congregation as having a more centralized power structure, the pastor acting as the dominant force involved in large and small decision making. McGaw describes the charismatic congregation as having a broader base of power, with elected elders performing in the role of assistant pastors. McGaw states "there is some indication that a centralized power structure in a congregation may lower the consensus and therefore diminish the sense of belonging and meaning." McGaw concludes that commitment is stronger in the charismatic congregation than in the mainline congregation with decentralization of authority being one contributing element.[31]

Other researchers examined the ambiguity of the lines of responsibility (lack of clarity) as a contributor to tension in non-profit organizations.[32] Members' access to the power structure in congregations was found to have a significant positive relationship to the percent of income contributed.[33] In my study of Reform Jewish congregations, for both leaders and members there was a significant and positive correlation between perceptions of empowerment and reputational effectiveness.[34] **In other words, the higher the reported level of feeling empowered, the higher the rating of reputational effectiveness. The feeling of being informed, included, and valued is an important factor in both leaders' and members' assessments of their congregation's ability to function effectively.[35]**

Summary of the Research—The research investigating organizational effectiveness provides strong evidence that these organizational behaviors are associated with the more effective nonprofit organizations:

♦ shared vision in mission statements, goals, and strategies arrived at in an inclusive process and shared with the members,

♦ boards that engage in ongoing educational experiences,

♦ boards that engage in ongoing self-evaluation,

♦ a more decentralized power structure with a membership that is empowered through clarity of responsibilities, shared information, and access to leadership.

The same behaviors are associated with more effective religious congregations.

GOVERNANCE

Structure – Most Reform Jewish congregations follow the hierarchical, business style structure with a governing board that hires the senior professional staff, oversees committees that report to the board, carry out most of the congregation's activities, and establishes policies for operating the organization. The details of this hierarchy are directed in the by-laws of the congregation.

The by-laws and policies set the tone for the workings of the congregation. If the by-laws and policies clearly describe the responsibilities of the officers and staff, provide for a succession plan for vice presidents, require open board meetings and an informed membership, and delineate a requirement for periodic by-laws review, many problems can be avoided, as follows:.

- There is less likelihood of territorial infighting among the leaders.

- The nominating committee is less likely to be scrambling to find a nominee for president in the months before a sitting president completes his or her term. In addition, the incoming president can prepare effectively to take over the responsibilities by working closely with the president, especially in the year before stepping into the position. The incoming president can also take advantage of training opportunities such as those provided by the URJ (e. g., URJ Biennial gatherings and the URJ Scheidt Seminar developed for just this purpose).

- Members of the congregation who have an interest in an issue before the board can attend the board meeting and, if specified in the by-laws, can voice their concern. This is an important factor in the empowerment of members.

- The by-laws will reflect the expectations of the leaders and members ensuring that it remains contemporary, meaningful, and useful.

Behaviors/Culture – The expectations established in the by-laws and policies should be known and followed by the leaders of the congregation. If all board members are provided with a notebook that includes the information they may need, including the by-laws, there is a greater likelihood that the guidelines in these documents will be respected. Other items that should be included in that notebook are the mission statement of the organization, a history of the congregation, a roster of the current board with contact information, a list of past presidents, a list of the Temple or church staff and contact information, a set of policies enacted by the board, and information regarding the URJ or other denominational structure.

Other behaviors of board members will also influence the culture of the congregation. Board members should be accessible to the membership, participating in congregational life as their time permits. When the board meeting agenda is set, the focus should be on setting policy and managing their fiduciary responsibilities, not on managing the day-to-day operations of the organization. Upcoming issues and board decisions should be reported to the congregation in an appropriate and timely manner.

Another behavior that influences the culture of the congregation is the expectation of the delegation of responsibilities. This applies most dramatically to chair positions. When an individual accepts the responsibility for leadership of a committee, program, project or task, all too often that person attempts to fulfill that responsibility alone. Perhaps, this chairperson believes that working alone is a more efficient way to do the job. Perhaps, this person believes that, by performing all the work him- or herself, he or she will have greater control of the outcome. Or maybe, he or she just thinks it's easier that way. Unfortunately, in most cases none of these beliefs is true. This chairperson is missing the point of "committee," the value of including others, and the opportunity for his or her own experience with leadership. The old expression, "two heads are better than one," is usually true and including other people in the process often provides a better result. And very importantly, including others creates a broader base for future leadership and a greater sense of connection and engagement for more members. Another outcome engendered by a "committee of one" is the greater likelihood of burn-out by that chairperson. Torah teaches us that delegating responsibilities is a demonstration of leadership (See Torah quote at the beginning of Chapter Two). As per the Torah quote, delegating responsibilities is leading Jewishly as is including Torah and Jewish values in decision making. In summary, it is the leadership, both professional and lay, that establishes the culture of the congregation. If the goal is to be a congregation based on relationships, every policy and every financial decision should reflect this value. Board decisions, made with knowledge of related Torah teachings and Jewish values, will help provide an understanding of the congregation's direction. And an atmosphere that demonstrates the valuing of openness, acceptance, and inclusion will go a long way in creating a culture of warmth and welcome.

GIVING OF THEIR TIME – A THEORETICAL PERSPECTIVE

Synagogues and churches are dependent on volunteers—unpaid workers by definition—to do much of the work of the organization. That very dependence requires that those volunteers find motivation other than the paycheck (which is often a large part of the motivation for paid workers in for-profit organizations) to provide time, effort, and funds necessary for the functioning of the organization. Complicating the need to motivate volunteers is the awareness that individuals are motivated by different things. "Different strokes for different folks!" The understanding of that diversity requires that various views of motivation be considered and brought into play.

A social theory is an explanation of human behavior. There are many theories regarding motivation that have been espoused over the decades of the 20th and 21st centuries. They come into and out of favor, are difficult to measure and quantify, and can be complicated and difficult to apply to many situations. For the purposes of this book, I will present two theories that, while considered old and even outdated, seem to help in understanding volunteer behavior, and have informed my own understanding of volunteer motivation.

Maslow's Hierarchy of Needs

As described by Chess and Norlin in the 1950s, Abraham Maslow developed the concept of a Hierarchy of Needs. He identified five genetic levels of need:

- survival,

- safety and security,

- social and belonging,

- esteem,

- self-actualization.

These needs are arranged in a hierarchy from the most basic to the most qualitative. The first four, arranged here in ascending order (survival, safety, belonging, and esteem) are considered basic needs. The survival need includes such things as air, water, and food, the physiological needs of the human body. Safety and security needs refer to seeking an environment that protects the person and his or her belongings. Social and belonging needs deal with relationships, the need to be loved. **"It is only through other people that our need for a sense of belongingness and love can be satisfied."**[36] Esteem needs include self-respect and the respect from others, a sense of competency and feeling good about oneself. Self-actualization, the highest level need in the hierarchy, is considered to be a meta need; it "transcends the basic needs of the individual and deal[s] with the capacity of the person to become all that he or she can be."[37] As described by Maslow, once a level is satisfied, the need loses its power to motivate and the next level gains domination.

Application of Maslow's hierarchy to congregational volunteerism, while more or less unconscious, is straight-forward. Participation in the life of a congregation occasionally may be related to meeting survival needs and security needs, but the relationship of Maslow's hierarchy to participation becomes more apparent in meeting the need for belonging, the need for esteem, and the need for self-actualization. Some individuals join a congregation and volunteer specifically to meet the need for belonging, to be a part of something. Some volunteer and become leaders because they are motivated by the need for esteem, to have others look up to them. And some are motivated at that metalevel of need satisfaction when their depth of involvement, skill development, and leadership represent "all that he or she can be,"—self-actualization.

Homans Social Exchange Theory

Also presented by Chess and Norlin, the Social Exchange Theory, as conceptualized by Homans in the 1950s, also holds meaning for dealing with volunteers in congregational life. Briefly stated, many human needs are met through the exchange of things, services, or sentiments based on **imprecise, unconscious, and uncalculated <u>perceived</u> value** [emphasis added] ultimately resulting in social organization. Furthermore, according to Homans, ". . . An exchange always involves both a cost and a reward to each person. Derived from this is the assumption that the relationship will be continued as long as the perceived costs of the exchange over time do not exceed its rewards, or that a more advantageous alternative is not available."[38] In order to maintain a relationship, the perceived "rewards," or benefits must be greater than the perceived "costs." "People make choices in what they do and what they won't do, with whom they associate and with whom they do not associate. They choose among alternatives based on expected benefits related to their own needs, past experiences and the range of options they believe are open to them."[39] Again, according to Homans' theory, these choices are unprecise, unconscious, and uncalculated.

With these concepts in mind, the volunteer in a congregation, who receives no monetary reward for his or her services, may choose to participate in the life or leadership of a congregation based on his or her perception of the "rewards" for that effort. I am not suggesting that the volunteer consciously calculates the value of their effort and the value of the "reward," but that there is an underlying, unconscious expectation of the exchange. In congregation life, the rewards might be extrinsic such as appreciation, recognition, or advancement. The "rewards" might be intrinsic such as increased knowledge, new skills or self-actualization. Leaders of congregations do well to be aware of the possible value of these rewards, providing appreciation, recognition, education, skill development, and advancement at appropriate levels to those whose participation is desired. Saying thank you in multiple venues, creating recognition opportunities, providing leadership development and board education programs, subsidizing attendance at seminars and conferences, and paying careful attention to past participation during the nominating process are all ways that "reward" congregational participation and leadership.

Based on the concepts of Social Exchange Theory, providing the "rewards" available in a congregational setting is not optional. There is an "obligation to reciprocate" when a volunteer provides a service or when a donor provides funds.[40] Given the dependence of congregations on volunteer support, providing appropriate rewards for those volunteers is essential to the formation and continuity of the congregation as a social organization. It is essential to the maintenance of the rewards over costs equation. If the "rewards" are ignored, and the "costs" are perceived as the experience of greater consequence, members will likely cease to participate or, worse yet, disassociate themselves from the congregation.

See Appendix 1B (pp. 96-97) for some suggestions of conditions conducive to the motivation of volunteers.

PROVIDING A VALUE BASIS FOR MANAGEMENT PRACTICES

The importance of empowering others has been recognized by leaders from Biblical times to present-day management gurus. As described at the beginning of Chapter Two in the Torah quote, Moses, acting on advice from his father-in-law, delegated authority to a hierarchy of judges. He decentralized the power in his community, including many others in the leadership of the people. Repeatedly, throughout the desert wanderings of the Israelites, Moses heeded the cry of the people (Numbers 11: 2,10-15; 14: 1-19) (See Torah quote at the beginning of Chapter Three). He took their needs seriously and responded on their behalf. He facilitated changes to meet their needs. He valued their perspective. He listened.

In his final address to the Israelites, Moses called together all the people, those of highest rank to the lowliest, ". . . your tribal heads, your elders and your officials, all the men of Israel, your children, your wives, even the stranger within your camp, from woodchopper to waterdrawer . . ." (See quote at the beginning of this chapter).[41] In this way Moses included and informed the whole community as he recounted their history and their obligations in their covenant with God. He gave them "a mind to understand," "eyes to see," and "ears to hear" (Deuteronomy 29:3)[42] In the words of Rabbi Plaut, Moses was "laying down an enduring foundation in that the Torah is declared to be valid for all generations, freely accessible to every member of the people, and not, as among other nations, the possession of a privileged few."[43]

Ezra, described "by tradition to be second in importance only to Moses,"[44] presented the teachings of Moses to the people at the water gate ". . .before the congregation, men and women and all who could listen with understanding," ". . . in the sight of all the people . . ." (Nehemiah 8:2 and 8: 5).[45] He took the teachings to the people on their own "turf," including them, bringing them into the circle of knowledge. But he did more than read to the people. He and other leaders with him made the effort to make sure the people understood what was being read to them. "They read from the scroll of the Teaching of God, translating it and giving the sense; so they understood the reading "(Nehemiah 8: 8).[46] He gave them not only the text but the context as well.

These Biblical leaders—by including all the people regardless of rank, by heeding and responding to the needs of the people, by sharing power, information, and knowledge—demonstrated a will to empower those who followed them. They provided the models for leading 'Jewishly.'

Today, those who write about organization management also recognize the value of leaders empowering their followers. Drucker approached the notion of empowerment: as follows: "Over the door to the non-profit's boardroom there should be an inscription that says: *Membership on this board is not power, it is responsibility.*"[47] In a conversation with Drucker, Max DePree described this responsibility in terms of debt:

> Leaders are given the gift of leadership by those who choose or agree to follow. We're basically a nation of volunteers. I think this means that people choose a leader to a great extent on the basis of what they believe the leader can contribute to the person's ability to achieve his or her goals in life. This puts the leader in the position of being indebted—in the sense of what he or she owes to the organization.[48]

Drucker further summarizes DePree's comments, stating

> . . .[The leaders] owe the customers, the clients, the constituency, whether they are parishioners, or patients, or students. They

owe the followers, whether that's faculty, or employees, or volunteers. And what they owe is really to enable people to realize their potential, to realize their purpose in serving the organization.[49]

As stated by Hesselbein, "The more power we give away, the more we have."[50]

The results of much of the organizational research support the teachings of these leaders, both Biblical and contemporary, providing empirical and value-based evidence that an educated and prepared congregational leadership and a congregational membership that feels included, informed, and valued— leadership and membership that is enabled and empowered—are associated with congregations that are perceived to be functioning effectively.

CONNECTING MANAGEMENT PRACTICES TO RELATIONAL JUDAISM

Participating in the life and leadership of a congregation should be a positive experience. Not that one should expect all experiences to be good, or happy, or easy, or even comfortable. There are bound to be times of disagreement, dissatisfaction, or disappointment. We cannot expect every program to succeed, every committee to stay in budget, everyone else to agree with our opinions, every member to be happy, or every relationship to be joyful. Anyone who has ever worked in a congregational setting knows that is not realistic. But when challenges arise, and arise they will, an understanding of healthy management principles, a sincere desire to find equitable solutions, and a desire to learn and grow from the experience can go a long way to providing positive outcomes. Knowing that the organization is striving to function in accordance with those principles that have been demonstrated to produce desirable results can establish a basis for working toward that positive experience.

And focusing on the relationships involved—member to member, member to congregation, member to his or her connection to the tenets of the faith— helps us to keep those challenges in line with our values. A relationship-based congregation does not measure success solely by the number of members, nor by the number of programs, nor by the number of people participating in programs, but rather by the quality of relationships developed among the members and by the quality of the members' relationship with the synagogue or church. This does not mean that congregational leaders will cease to be aware of the quantitative measures. It means that these leaders will also be aware that the numbers alone do not tell the whole story. For example, an increase in the number of member units (singles and families) reflects both the number of new member units and the number of member units resigning from the congregation. In a relational congregation, leaders also pay close attention to what attracted the new members, and the reasons members resigned. This change in focus moves the mindset from being a quantitative one to a qualitative one, which is more reflective of the values a religious congregation represents. And members who feel that their need for connecting and belonging is met by their participation in the life of the congregation are more likely to describe their experience in that congregation as fulfilling their needs, serving the members competently, and satisfying them spiritually. In other words, they are more likely to view their congregation to be a more effective organization.

CHAPTER TWO

BERESHEIT – IN THE BEGINNING

But Moses' father-in-law said to him, "The thing you are doing is not right; you will surely wear yourself out, and these people as well. For the task is too heavy for you; Now listen to me. I will give you counsel, and God be with you! You represent the people before God: you bring the disputes before God, and enjoin upon them the laws and the teachings, and make known to them the way they are to go and the practices they are to follow. You shall also seek out from among all the people capable men who fear God, trustworthy men who spurn ill-gotten gain. Set these over them as chiefs of thousands, hundreds, fifties, and tens, and let them judge the people at all times. Have them bring every major dispute to you, but let them decide every minor dispute themselves. Make it easier for yourself by letting them share the burden with you. If you do this—and so God commands—you will be able to bear up; and all these people too will go home unwearied." Moses headed his father-in-law and did just as he had said.[1]

Exodus: 18: 17-24, translation from TANAKH

THE VISION

The Rabbi and the President – Early in 2013 at Temple Shalom, in Naples, Florida, the president and the rabbi, Adam Miller, were in the habit of meeting to discuss congregational issues. They shared their concerns. The president at that time was an attorney who described his law practice as "relational law." He believed this concept could apply to our Temple. Rabbi Miller was concerned that the congregation was focusing too heavily on programming rather than on people or the reasons we exist as a congregation. Both of these leaders sensed that there was a need for a shift in congregational thinking and direction.

Rabbi Miller had read Simon Sinek's book *Start with Why*.[2] Sinek's basic concept is that the '*why* we do what we do' is what motivates us and those around us. Inspired leadership starts with understanding and sharing the *why*. The Rabbi gave the book to the president to read, and the two men discussed its application to Temple. The president held a Board retreat that focused on the concepts of the Sinek book. The Rabbi and the president began asking the other congregation leaders, when they were discussing and deliberating their various decisions, to start with the question, "Why are we here?" and "Why are we doing this" as compared to, "What do we do?" They were attempting to stimulate a new way of thinking.

Perhaps because his own thinking had already taken the "Start with Why" direction, Rabbi Miller was open to a new paradigm. When attending a convention of the Central Conference of American Rabbis, in March 2013, he heard Dr. Ron Wolfson's presentation. Dr. Wolfson's book, *Relational Judaism: Using the Power of Relationships to Transform the Jewish Community*, had just been published. Dr. Wolfson's rationale and stories resonated for Rabbi Miller, furthering his sense that we at Temple Shalom were "missing the mark." Rabbi Miller read Dr. Wolfson's book, shared the ideas with our congregation 's president, and gave him a copy of the book to read. Almost immediately, the Rabbi and the President of Temple Shalom agreed to begin a journey of change.

Knowing that such a journey would not be easy or swift and that the support of the congregation 's leadership would be essential, they began by courting the support of the Temple Board and other influential individuals. Rabbi Jonah Pesner, then Vice President of the Union for Reform Judaism, was brought to Naples to speak to the group of Temple leaders. He led the group in a process of sharing stories, listening to each other, and learning an appreciation of the value of listening and connecting to one another. Shortly after that gathering, every

Board member and other congregational leaders, including my husband Neil and me, were given a copy of Dr. Wolfson's book. We were all urged to read it. We became familiar with Dr. Wolfson's Twelve Principles of Relational Engagement (my abbreviated interpretation can be found in Appendix 2A, pp. 98-99). Over the next few months, the acceptance and support of the concepts of Relational Judaism by the lay leadership grew.

Because of my earlier experiences learning about relationship-based congregation (see Introduction), it was clear to me that Dr. Wolfson's focus on relationships had similar underpinnings as the earlier work of Rabbi Richard Address, who was then with the Union for Reform Judaism. (Rabbi Address had written his doctoral dissertation on the sacredness of relationships and had envisioned congregations based on that value. Several congregations in various parts of the U.S. had been designated as pilot congregations, and each had developed their own model of such a congregation.) Having been introduced to one of the pilot congregation's model of a relationship-based congregation at a URJ Regional Biennial gathering many years earlier, I had already embraced the concept. And just as I had felt all those years earlier, I knew I wanted to be part of a congregation that reflected the values of Relational Judaism.

Seeing there was interest in moving our Temple in a meaningful direction, I gave Rabbi Miller a copy of a one-page handout I had prepared many years earlier for the leaders of another congregation. The handout was my brief interpretation of a relationship-based congregation as developed by Rabbi Address. Soon thereafter, Rabbi Miller, with the agreement of the president, asked Neil and me to chair the change process, a Relational Judaism Initiative, at Temple Shalom. With pleasure, we accepted the challenge.

SHARING THE VISION

Where to begin? That was the question! Neil and I had been charged with the responsibility of introducing the concept of Relational Judaism to our congregation and implementing a process that would reflect those relational values. But truth be told, we weren't sure **how** to do that! We knew we needed to get the attention of our members. We needed to explain what we were doing, why we were doing it, and how it would benefit the members.

The two of us did a lot of talking and brainstorming. We listened to others and sorted out ideas. It was "messy" and haphazard at the beginning. Our process at that time, as well as the discussions between the two of us, were not in any way formal or organized, but we did develop some basic understandings. We felt that:

1. Whatever we did had to "fit" our congregation—our culture, our time-line, our needs. It must take into consideration our demographics and our history. We would not in any way be replacing the structure or leadership that existed; we would be working within the structure and working closely with the leaders and staff.

2. We needed to be inclusive, involving as many people as possible in our process. We had learned from experience that the greater the involvement of each individual, the greater the depth of buy-in. And the more people involved in the process and its development, the greater the attendance and participation at events and programs. Both depth and breadth require the involvement of many members, especially at the beginning.

3. The participation in the process had to be intergenerational from the beginning. Because our congregation was often divided along generational lines, involving members from the various age groups was vital. Not only did overall participation need to be intergenerational, but within groups—as much as possible—there had to be a mix of generations.

4. The initial introduction to the congregation had to be attention catching, upbeat, and memorable. It had to reflect a positive plan and feel like a warm embrace! The introductory experience must feel valuable, doable, and joyful!

To further develop a plan of action, and to begin involving more members, a Relational Judaism Team was formed. To get started, we asked people we knew and people the Rabbi recommended to be a part of the Team. We began publicizing that we were forming a Team (Appendix 2B, p. 100). We held our first meeting on October 27, 2013, with about thirty Team members in attendance. We opened our agenda with a *D'var Torah* (a Torah teaching) that tells us how we are to treat strangers (Appendix 2C, p. 101). Appendices 2D and 2E (p. 102 and p. 103) are the agenda for that first meeting and the outcomes we wanted to achieve.

As Neil and I continued to discuss our options, we frequently referred to Dr. Wolfson's book for ideas and guidance. One evening in November, when we were feeling frustrated by our lack of an opening plan or event, it occurred to Neil that having Dr. Wolfson visit us and address the congregation might be just the start we needed. Without hesitation, Neil called the author to see if such a thing were possible. Sure enough, by the end of the conversation, we had a plan and a possible date!

After the usual issues of clearing the date on the Temple and community calendars and securing funding, we were off and running. Dr. Wolfson would come to our Temple on a Sunday morning early in February (which was Super Bowl Sunday! Oy!) and speak to our members, explaining the importance of relationships to the well-being of the congregation. We would then provide a lunch (underwritten by a generous member) to be served at no charge to the attendees immediately after religious school and our program. And, speaking of the religious school, we planned to conclude the program part of the morning with the children of the religious school singing several upbeat melodies, serenading the attendees, and leading us into the social hall for lunch.

Knowing we had only about six weeks to pull this event together, we enlisted the time and efforts of our Relational Judaism Team and the support of Temple staff. Working together, we arranged publicity (lots of it! See Appendix 2F, pp. 104-105, for sample articles), program planning, catering, table decorations, room arrangements and coordination with the Religious School Director. Each area required groups of volunteers, leaders, and workers. Most groups were intergenerational and almost everyone we asked to help agreed to do so.

In addition to articles in our monthly bulletin, save-the-date flyers, weekly e-blasts, *Shabbat* handouts and remarks by Rabbi Miller and Board members from the *bimah*, phone calls were made to every member household (about four hundred fifty households!) by members of the Relational Judaism Team and Board Members. We wanted to convey to the members of the congregation the importance of the event and the enthusiasm of the leaders .

Our opening event proved to be exciting, filling our sanctuary with over three hundred congregants. The event lived up to our expectations and more. Many of those who attended the program were the parents of the religious school students, our younger generation of members. We also had strong representation from our empty nesters, retirees, and older members. (Because we are located in a sunbelt/resort area community, we have a larger than usual population of retirees and senior citizens, both full-time residents and "snowbirds.") While we were very pleased with the response, we understood that we had a long way to go for many of our members to really "get" the concept of Relational

Judaism. Even those who attended the kick-off event would need a lot more information and experience living in a relationship-based congregation to fully embrace the meaning.

DEVELOPING THE VISION

We scheduled our first post-event meeting one week after the opening event and another meeting on the following Sunday. We invited the whole congregation to join our Team. Fueled by Rabbi Miller's and Board members' remarks from the *Bimah*, monthly Bulletins articles, Shabbat handout articles, and word of mouth, our Team had doubled in size to about sixty members! In Appendix 2G (pp. 106-108) are the bulletin articles inviting all members to participate (an invitation we have repeated frequently throughout our process).

In those early meetings, both before and after our kick-off event, we agreed on a name for our initiative—One Family! We immediately began using this name for our process and our Team. We also:

- Planned a workshop for the Team and Board members. The agenda for this workshop is presented in Appendix 2H (pp. 109-110).

- Planned for collection and a review of data from member applications, surveys, and our database.

- Planned for Action Groups with leaders for each project.

The process for developing action plans and specific Action Groups began with "brainstorming" sessions. After everyone's ideas were written on a flip chart, we prioritized them based on which ideas were immediately doable, which ideas would have immediate impact, which ideas had a passionate following, and which ideas were cost feasible. Chapter Three provides more detail regarding this process and the outcomes.

As organization and management people, Neil and I think in terms of setting goals and establishing measurable outcomes. Working with the Rabbi and our Team, we developed our transformation initiative goals as follows:

- To increase connectivity and engagement among our members;

- To build and develop relationships for current, new, and potential members;

- To create an intergenerational bridge.

We created a set of desired outcomes as follows:

- Increased involvement in the life of Temple Shalom
- Increase in positive talk about Temple Shalom
- Increase in hits to the Temple sites
- Increase in membership
- Increase in donations to specific projects
- Improved financial stability

While some of these outcomes would not be readily measurable (e.g., increase in positive talk about Temple Shalom) and not all are relational in nature (e.g., improved financial stability), these are the outcomes that our brainstorming process produced.

With outcomes in place, we were poised to establish baseline data (data developed before introducing new initiatives). Information such as membership numbers, attendance numbers, and financial status were and are readily available. However, determining how people feel about the Temple, their views about how well the Temple meets their needs, would require a survey. Because our leaders had recently been advised by outside consultants to avoid surveys, and an unrelated survey that had been done a few years earlier, there was a lack of support among the leadership for conducting a survey prior to the launch of our process. I had hoped that some data from that earlier survey would prove useful as baseline satisfaction information. Unfortunately, due to the nature of the questions, I soon learned this was not the case. While still firmly believing in the importance of baseline satisfaction data, I accepted that a pre-Relational Judaism survey would not be done. The evaluation part of our One Family process is described in detail in Chapter Seven.

The enthusiasm at our opening event and our early meetings was encouraging. We had a sense we were on the right track. But still, we knew that implementing a transformation was a big deal. We soon learned that it was the creativity and passion of our One Family Team and our Temple membership that would move us forward.

CHAPTER THREE

IMPLEMENTATION – BRINGING THE TRANSFORMATION TO LIFE

> The people took to complaining bitterly before the Lord. The Lord heard and was incenced; a fire of the Lord broke out against them, ravaging the outskirts of the camp. The people cried out to Moses. Moses prayed to the Lord, and the fire died down.[1]
>
> Numbers 11: 1-2, translation from TANAKH

So . . . We were off to a great start! But where do we go from here? Besides having no real blueprint to follow, we had a huge challenge—no budget! Because the Relational Judaism planning had begun in the middle of a fiscal year **after the budgeting for the year was in place,** our process had not been allotted any funds. All expenses we incurred for our kick-off event had been underwritten by donations. But we forged ahead, knowing we had the support of our leadership and believing strongly this direction was right for our congregation.

Beginning one week after our opening event, meetings of the Relational Judaism Team were held in February and March 2014. Just as Moses listened to the pleas of the people, took their needs seriously, and acted on their behalf (see Torah quote above), we knew we must listen to the needs and ideas of our members. Each time we met and between meetings as well, we were aware of the need to listen and be open to new ideas. So, we began by listening. Brainstorming and updates were always included as agenda items at our meetings. We were looking for steps we could take immediately and some things we could plan for the future. We were looking for both immediate impact and long-term change. Among the early meeting outcomes was the naming of our process. The Rabbi had suggested calling our process "One Family." This name was proposed to our team, and they liked it. One Family became the name by which our process was known, by which our team was known, and, over time, has become associated with our Temple. One Family represents who we are and what we strive to be!

Rather than creating more programs, we saw our task as creating systems and environments that promote members engaging with each other. After the kick-off event, our focus was—and still is—not attracting large numbers, but small group opportunities to make connections and engage with one another and individual opportunities to connect to Temple. The brainstorming done by our Team in those early meetings resulted in this list of doable "action items:"

- Home-held *Shabbat* dinners
- *Shabbat* ambassadors (later known as *Shalom Chaverim*)
- Name badges
- New member integration
- Exit interviews
- Affinity groups
- Communications
- Intergenerational events
- Changes in physical plant (planning for later implementation)

Priorities were established based on immediate or long-term impact, 'doability,' team member interest, and financial feasibility. These projects were chosen to begin our process of change:

- Home-held *Shabbat* dinners
- Name badges
- Affinity groups
- New member integration
- Changes in physical plant

Over the next few weeks, members of the One Family Team signed up for their choice or choices of projects, forming Action Groups for each project. Leaders emerged, and interested volunteers came forward. Each group held meetings, researched ideas and planned for their project. Over the next five years, the projects began, some were completed, adjustments were made as needed, and others (that were ongoing) have become part of the fiber of our congregation. Some projects, after what seemed like successful beginnings, fizzled out. Periodic reports to the congregation regarding the progress of our Team have appeared in our monthly bulletin and annual meeting reports. The One Family Team met annually for the first three years, evaluating progress, and considering new ideas. Additional projects emerged from these meetings:

- Technology enhancements

- One Family . . . Many Stories (one-on-one conversations)

- *Shalom Chaverim* (Welcome Friends) (formerly called Ambassadors)

The pages of this chapter describe the projects and changes introduced or furthered by our One Family Team, our lay leadership, and our Rabbi.

NAME BADGES

One early meeting of the One Family Team produced the idea of name badges for all adult Temple members of the congregation. Our Team enthusiastically embraced this idea—we really do not all know each other! It was obvious at our *Erev Shabbat Onegs* (social gatherings after Friday evening Sabbath services) that attendees gathered in groups of friends, sitting at round tables in "closed" circles. Some Team members reported being ill-at-ease approaching people they did not know, unsure of whether the person was a guest or member. Others reported discomfort because they had difficulty remembering names. The result is what appears to be an unfriendly environment—guests in a room of seemingly closed groups. We did have a guest table with brochures of information about Temple and, usually, there was a membership committee representative nearby to greet the guests. However, this apparently wasn't enough to make people feel welcome. Many of us had heard at one time or another that people who had attended services and stayed for the *Oneg* found ours to be an "unfriendly" congregation. Obviously, change was needed!

We agreed as a group that, in addition to some other changes (see *Shalom Chaverim* in this chapter and Audacious Hospitality, Chapter Four), name

badges could help us provide a more welcoming atmosphere. One member of the Team offered to cover the cost of the badges. Another Team member volunteered to research the best type of badge for us. Another Team member, who owned a woodworking company, volunteered to have a cabinet built to hold the badges. Research was done to determine the best type of badge that would meet our needs, and the badges were ordered.

Meanwhile, a beautiful and versatile cabinet was built.

The badges were arranged alphabetically in the cabinet drawers. Shortly before Rosh Hashonah, 2014, the badges and cabinet were introduced to the congregation. Because we envisioned our members accessing their badges from the cabinet as they entered the building, we started by providing assistance with locating the badges in the drawers. We asked them to drop the badges in baskets as they left. We continued in this manner with members of the Action Group volunteering each week to re-file the badges from the baskets into the cabinet drawers. After about six weeks, we asked the attendees to re-file their own badges. The transition went smoothly, and our members soon became accustomed to locating and returning their badges, not only for services but whenever they came into the building for events. This practice continues to this day.

After the member badges were well accepted, special name badges were provided to guests attending services. These badges are different in appearance from the members' badges. While some guests refuse the badges, many more accept them. These guest badges are very helpful in identifying the visitors, providing members with the information they need to ensure that visitors are welcomed.

Another way the name badges could be useful is the easy identification of new members. We are considering adding an easily removable sticker to the new member badges. With these in place, we will know that these individuals might need to be introduced and connected to other members.

The feedback regarding name badges from our members has been very positive! The badges were well received and continue to be much appreciated. This project has been one of our great successes! When new members join the congregation, their name badges are prepared immediately (in house). They seem genuinely pleased to receive them and look forward to finding their own badges in the cabinet.

DESIRED OUTCOMES

1. Development of a friendlier atmosphere at *Oneg Shabbats* and other gatherings.

2. Easier identification of guests at *Oneg Shabbat* and other gatherings.

3. Easier identification of new members at *Oneg Shabbat* and other gatherings.

4. Reductions of barriers among members (i.e., reluctance to approach one another) creating easier connections among members.

SHABBAT DINNERS

Another early project to be implemented was home-held *Shabbat* Dinners. With one couple chairing and organizing this project, we began with articles in our monthly bulletin (Appendix 3A-1, p. 111), our weekly eblast, our *Shabbat* service handout (Appendix 3A-2, p. 112), and comments from the *bimah*. Members of the congregation were asked if they would like to host a *Shabbat* dinner or attend a *Shabbat* dinner in another member's home. In addition, the Rabbi identified some members we could draw into Temple participation. Hosts set the number of invitees, usually six to ten people. Because the goal was to develop new relationships, the hosts were encouraged to invite some people they did not know, or know well, along with their own friends. The Chairs worked with the volunteer hosts in developing their list of invitees. A sample script was provided

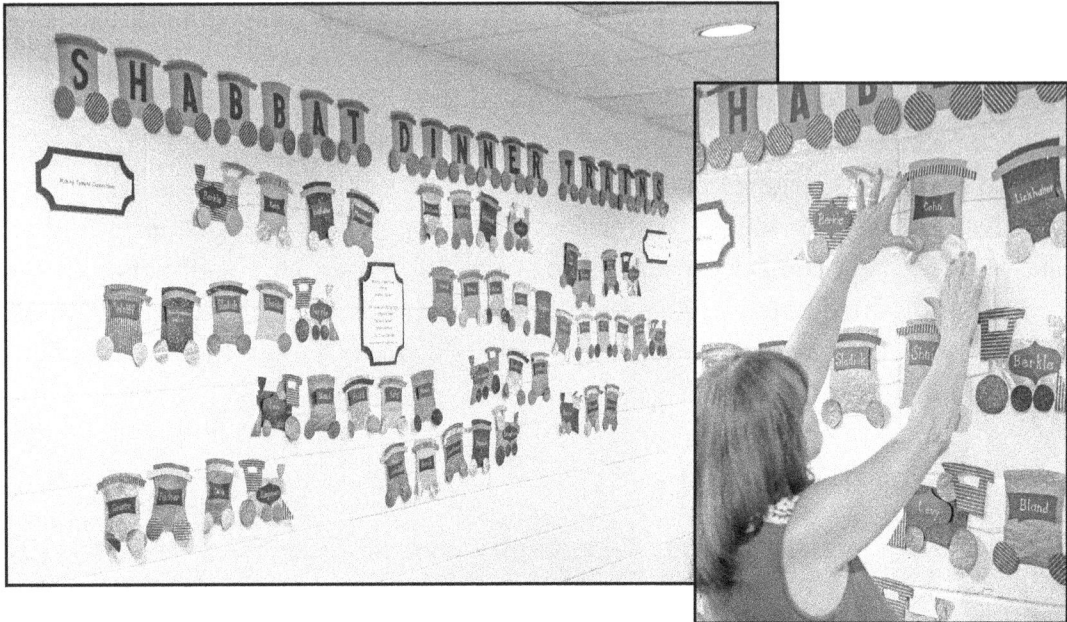

for the hosts to use when making phone call invitations (Appendix 3A-3, p. 113). Hosts were encouraged to have a dinner that was comfortable for them—traditional *Shabbat*, pot luck, barbeque, etc.

While hosts were provided with some suggested ways to celebrate *Shabbat* (Appendix 3A-4, pp. 114-118), they did not have to follow the suggestions. Further, to keep the evening from being rushed and to allow time for the host and invitees to get to know one another, to develop relationships, there was no expectation to attend services at Temple that evening.

Every *Shabbat* Dinner held was different and had its own "flavor." Both hosts and guests reported finding the experience rewarding and fun. Members that might not otherwise have had the experience of knowing one another enjoyed discovering common interests—new relationships developed! Some of those that were guests at another's home then volunteered to host dinners of their own. When those who have shared one of these Shabbat dinners see fellow diners at services or Temple events, they have a new basis for conversation and fellowship.

After a while, when interest in home-held *Shabbat* dinners waned, an attempt was made to revitalize that interest. Among the efforts to do this, was a plan to make the project more visible. We began a process called "*Shabbat* Dinners with Strings Attached." An article explaining the project appeared in our monthly bulletin (Appendix 3A-5, p. 119). The trains, with host names on the engines and guest names on the cars, are shown above.

While the *Shabbat* Dinner project had a strong beginning, interest waned after the first year and a half, and for three years we could not revitalize it. Our *Shabbat* Dinner Trains did not stimulate the additional interest we had hoped for. During those three years, we were unable to find a new chair when one was needed. Unfortunately, our *Shabbat* Dinner project came to a standstill.

Because we very much wanted to revitalize this project, we continued to search for a new chair. In the spring of 2018, a member came forward who was interested in reviving the home *Shabbat* Dinners. She quickly held a *Shabbat* Dinner in her home and had discussions with the previous chair. As of this writing, she is getting started. Her article in our *Shabbat Shalom* weekly handout is in Appendix 3A-6 (p. 120) and her article in our monthly *Voice* is in Appendix 3A-7 (p. 121). The project was given a new name, *Shabbat* Tables, and a new brochure was developed (Appendix 3A-8, pp. 122-127). An event was held to restart the project (a pot-luck *Shabbat* dinner before services) and new interest is developing.

DESIRED OUTCOMES

1. Strengthening of relationships among our congregants.
2. Development of new relationships among our congregants.
3. Involving members who have previously not been engaged in Temple life.

AFFINITY GROUPS

In the early meetings of the One Family Team, it was clear that the formation of affinity groups was desired. While affinity groups can be organized based on various types of similarities—demographics, interests, occupations, etc.—it was demographic affinity groups that were proposed at that time, empty nesters and senior singles, in particular. While neither was formed in the first year, two leaders came forward to organize the Empty Nesters Affinity Group. About two years into our One Family Initiative, it became clear that another affinity group was needed—an Interfaith Families Affinity Group.

Empty Nesters – During the first year of the One Family Initiative, the leaders of the Empty Nester Affinity Group developed a list of members of our congregation who fit this demographic. They had several tools for identifying these individuals and couples—our (then somewhat incomplete) database, our Temple directory, notices in our monthly Temple bulletin and Shabbat handout, reports from the Many Stories project, iTemple requests for responses, personal knowledge of our membership, and, of course, word of mouth. With assistance from our Membership Chair and our Concierge (more on this person later), a list was developed (and continues to grow). Communications began in that first year of One Family. In the second year, six couples came together for the first planning meeting. They brainstormed a list of possible programs and planned the first events—a *Seder* Leftovers potluck dinner and a sunset cruise from one of our local docks. The events were a great success! While the group has not met recently, new leadership is developing ideas for the future.

Senior Singles – For some time before the beginning of the One Family Initiative, a small group of single senior members of the Temple had been asking for programming designed for them. When this did not occur, they organized a group of their own outside the auspices of the Temple. This group is comprised of Temple members and other Jewish single seniors from the community. They had been meeting and planning for about a year when their request was raised at our One Family Team meeting. While we would have been happy to have this group functioning as a Temple-sponsored group, we agreed during this meeting not to interfere with an already functioning group.

Interfaith Families – About two years into the One Family Initiative, through the Many Stories project (later in this chapter), it became clear that there was another demographic group in our membership whose needs were not being adequately addressed—our interfaith families. We are currently planning to organize this group.

DESIRED OUTCOMES

1. Creation of opportunities for relationships among members with similar interests based on demographics.
2. Strengthening of relationships among our congregants.

WELCOMING NEW MEMBERS

Before the One Family Initiative, new members had been warmly received into our congregation. Our Membership Chair (who became a co-chair of One Family in 2015) wrote notes of welcome and made phone calls personally connecting with each new member individual or family. She arranged a New Member Sabbath complete with a potluck *Shabbat* Dinner prior to services. During services on that Shabbat, Rabbi Miller called all the new members to the *Bimah* for a blessing.

When we began our One Family Initiative, we added new aspects to our welcome to help integrate new members into the life of the congregation—the addition to the staff of the Concierge and a New Members Orientation event.

Membership Engagement Coordinator and Concierge—When prospective members approach Temple Shalom, their first contact is usually with our Concierge. This staff person greets them on the phone and in person, answers initial questions, takes them on a tour of the building, and introduces them to some other members of the staff. One of those staff members is our Executive Director who discusses our membership plan with them. The Concierge often invites the prospective member to services and an event, giving them opportunities to meet our members and to become familiar with our community. When the individual or family makes the commitment to become a part of our family, our Concierge and our Membership Chair (staff and lay leader) begin a process of assisting the new member's integration.

Throughout the first year of membership and, of course, throughout their membership, the new member can call on the Concierge to assist them in making connections at Temple Shalom. The Membership Chair continues all that she had done in the past and participates in arranging the New Members Orientation.

New Member Orientation – In November or December, a New Members Orientation was arranged on a weekday evening or just before *Erev Shabbat* services in our newly renovated Library. For this event, all staff members, the congregation President, and other lay leaders were present. After wine and cheese were served, and a little time for schmoozing, the staff and lay leaders were introduced, with new members introducing themselves. Some general information was provided about the congregation including an explanation of our One Family Initiative. The new members were given an opportunity to ask questions. The staff then dispersed to their work locations, and the lay leaders took small groups of the new members on a tour of the facility. When the groups arrived at each of the work locations, the staff member provided a brief presentation about what they do and how the space is used. After the tour, we again gathered in the Library for further questions and more schmoozing. The purpose of this orientation is to increase the comfort level of the new members, familiarizing them with who we are as a congregation, our physical plant, and who does what in the life of Temple Shalom. Another very important aspect of this event is to introduce the new members to each other, to give them an opportunity to play a little "Jewish geography"—to develop new relationships.

A year after the Concierge came on staff, the "tour" part of our orientation was not needed. The Concierge was already doing this with new and prospective members during their early contacts. The New Member Orientation was replaced with several wine and cheese events throughout the year for new members prior to *Erev Shabbat* services to continue providing opportunities for new members to get to know one another. Also, in addition to the potluck dinner on New Member Sabbath, another new member potluck dinner has been added to the calendar.

DESIRED OUTCOMES

1. Creation of relationships among new members.

2. Creation of relationships between our new members and our "old" members.

3. Enhancement of new members' familiarity with the staff and the facility.

4. Enhancement of sense of welcoming and integration of new members.

CHANGES IN PHYSICAL PLANT

When considering changes to our facility, our building, and grounds, our focus is on ensuring there are spaces where people can converse and connect, where relationships can develop.

The Library—Before we began our One Family initiative, a plan had been initiated to renovate our Temple library—a whole new look. Because the timing was so close to the work our One Family Team was doing, and because our library was a space that could be conducive to conversation and connection, it soon came to be thought of as one of our projects. In truth, our Team had little to do with the library project, but we were looking for the Library to be a conversation-friendly space. The Library project was designed and funded by a local furniture company owned by members of the congregation.

When the Library was completed, anyone would have thought that our Team had designed the room! In addition to a large table area for small meetings, there

◄ Seating Area

▲ The Temple Bean

◄ Meeting Area

are several upholstered, comfortable chairs where people can meet and talk, tables that seat four people (game table size), and a coffee bar (known as The Temple Bean!). The look of the room is attractive and welcoming. The room has new carpeting, new window treatments, and new shelving. It is light and bright and "easy on the eye!"

This welcoming and comfortable space was designed for meeting and gathering in various configurations for small group connections. The coffee bar, provides a warm incentive to sit and chat with others who are there. This has become apparent on weekdays when small group meetings are held in the library and when a group of women meets in the library to play *Mah Jongg*. It is also apparent on Sunday mornings while the children are attending Religious School. Before the advent of the Temple Bean, it was customary for parents to drop children at the Temple door and drive a mile down the road to a coffee shop to gather and chat until it was time to pick up their kids. When our library renovation and redecoration was being planned, this coffee shop closed. The leadership of Temple Shalom seized on the opportunity to develop our own space for coffee and chat. Thus, our Temple Shalom Temple Bean came into being. Many parents who had driven down the road during those Religious School hours stayed at Temple to schmooze!

So, it is no surprise that the Library has become a favorite space for small group gatherings. It also represents the broad concept of One Family . . . all that we plan and all that we do at Temple Shalom is done with the concept of Relational Judaism—One Family—in mind. We are not so concerned about territory, transactions, or who did what; our focus is on providing relational experiences and opportunities for our members. This beautiful room is a constant reminder we are in the midst of a transformation based on relationships.

Tribute Garden – Before the One Family Initiative was launched, a few One Family Team members with a passion for gardening and landscaping had expressed concern about a garden space outside our Social Hall. This space, visible at the front of our building, had not been productive for many years. Other than providing the location for our *Succah* in the past, the area was unused. The bushes that surrounded it were overgrown and unruly. Tree roots had caused damage to paved areas. The lawn was patchy and weedy. This outdoor space, located near our front door, was certainly in need of improvement.

In the early meetings of the One Family Team, these concerned members identified a group of people who might be interested in doing something with that space. They formed an Action Group and organized a meeting. The project planning got underway. It had been established at the outset that there was no budget to renovate the garden and, due to the Temple's tight financial situation, little likelihood of budgeted funds in the near future. However, because there was a good deal of planning to be done before spending any money, it was felt this Action Group should proceed anyway. So, the work of this Group was begun knowing that it could be quite a while before the project was implemented. To our great pleasure, over the next year as the planning proceeded, members with related resources offered both money and a landscaping company to do the job. The work on this space was implemented one and a half years into the One Family Initiative. The renovation included removing most of the existing lawn, foliage, and pavement and installing new bushes, trees, sod, gates, pavers, and benches to create a beautiful garden (shown here and featured on the front cover of this book).

After allowing time for the plants to grow and fill in, a dedication ceremony was held on April 2, 2017. The Temple Building and Grounds Committee determined and announced the levels of donations required to honor or memorialize someone with the "purchase" of a bench, a rock, a plant, or a paver thus creating a tribute garden. The publicity with this information soon followed, and that aspect of the project began. About three years into our One Family Initiative, not only had an unusable space been cleaned up and a garden created for engaging in quiet conversation or contemplation, but a fundraising opportunity had been developed! (See Appendix 3B, pp. 128-129.) This project was certainly a win-win-win for the Temple. This space near the front entrance to our Temple home was renovated, an environment conducive to making connections (and usable for some events) was created, and an on-going fundraiser was established.

DESIRED OUTCOMES

1. Creation of conversation-friendly spaces at Temple Shalom, providing enhanced opportunities for relationship development.

2. Provision of incentives for our members to "hang out" at Temple.

3. Creation of a beautiful, usable and productive space from an unusable space.

4. Creation of a fundraising opportunity.

TECHNOLOGY

Streaming Video – Several of our members expressed interest in providing streaming video of our religious services. The idea was researched and deemed feasible in our Sanctuary. All of the equipment needed including the video camera and computer for this system was made possible by the generosity of our members. The installation was done in-house. (The Temple pays a monthly fee to a streaming service.) Installation was completed, and the streaming video was introduced to the congregation in the summer of 2015, one and a half years after the launch of our One Family Initiative.

Since then, most religious services and events that take place in our sanctuary are recorded. Many are streamed live and are accessible through a link on our Temple website. Based on the reports from our members, the availability of *Shabbat* and holiday services is much appreciated by those members who cannot be at Temple due to illness or distance. (Many of our members are away for the summer and many travel throughout the year.) The videos are also archived enabling our members to view services and events from wherever they are and whenever they want.

iTemple and Techie Tutors – iTemple, a social networking service, was set up to be our Temple online community. All Temple members could access this platform. Members could create their own profiles, identify their interests, develop groups based on commonalities, and communicate with all the members on iTemple. This system enhanced our members' abilities to connect and engage with one another. The funds to purchase the platform on which iTemple is based, like most of the projects we undertook, were provided separately from our budgeted funds.

To work out kinks in the system, the service was made available to the members and staff in a series of small steps beginning in the fall of 2015. First the Board, then the staff, then the Religious School teachers and parents used the system. Finally, it was made available to the whole congregation in February 2016 (Appendix 3C, p. 130). When it became clear that many members were reluctant to use the system, a series of small seminars were arranged to assist the members. These seminars were arranged and taught by staff and a group of technologically savvy members we called Techie Tutors.

The structure for Techie Tutors had been set up a year earlier with a very different expectation. The original idea was to have our tech-savvy teens work with our older members who had difficulty using their technology—computers, notepads, and cell phones. We had envisioned the teens and older members meeting at Temple, and we had hopes of creating intergenerational connections as well as providing a valuable learning opportunity for our members. (Our older members often quipped "When I need help with my technology, I just ask my grandchildren!") We also believed that the teens could earn community service credits required by area high schools. While this seemed to us to be a win-win arrangement, it didn't work. There was little interest shown by either group— teens or older members.

When the issues arose regarding members not using iTemple, we adjusted the plan for our Techie Tutors. We asked tech-savvy adult members to assist other adult members and set up the seminars, beginning in the summer of 2016. Unfortunately, once again, little interest was shown in iTemple or the Techie Tutor plan. In the summer of 2017, the original platform for iTemple was discontinued, and a plan was made to explore an alternative social networking service. At the time of this writing, there is no immediate plan to reinstitute a Temple Shalom platform.

Hearing Loop – A "hearing loop" is a system for individuals with a hearing impairment who wear hearing aids equipped with a telecoil switch (originally designed for use with telephones). The loop provides quality sound amplification consistent with individual hearing capabilities and free from background noise (scuffling, coughing, paper shuffling, etc.). The system is comprised of a wire loop hidden under the carpet and is connected to the microphones. This wire encircles a space and transmits sound electromagnetically directly from microphones to personal hearing aids within the encircled space.

We began this project by researching the experiences of churches, synagogues, auditoriums, and other facilities already using the hearing loop. We checked into the feasibility and costs of installing a hearing loop in our sanctuary. After determining that our sanctuary is technologically compatible with a loop system and after obtaining the blessing of our Temple Board, we placed an article in our monthly bulletin describing the plan and requesting financial support (Appendix 3D-1, p. 131). Sisterhood and Men's Club were approached and both generously provided funds. Generous individuals also contributed funds. Before the loop was installed, more than half the costs were covered. Our system was installed in our sanctuary in August of 2016.

Soon after the loop was installed, we placed another article in our monthly bulletin (Appendix 3D-2, p. 132). Some of the same donors contributed additional funds, and a few other donors came forward to contribute. The remaining costs were covered.

Four headsets compatible with the loop system were purchased for those whose hearing aids were not compatible with the loop and for those who do not have hearing aids. (In addition, the headsets for the FM amplification system, formerly used, continue to function and are also available, if needed.) A statement regarding the availability of the hearing loop was inserted into our Shabbat handout and continues to appear there weekly (Appendix 3D-3, p. 133). An orientation program was held before the High Holidays to assist our congregants interested in making use of this loop. A practicing audiologist, holding a doctorate and certification by the American Speech, Hearing, and Language Association, was present to answer questions and to help our hearing aid users determine if their hearing aids were compatible with the loop. Another similar orientation program was held in January 2017, for our members who are only here in winter. The response has been very positive with statements of appreciation and reports that the sound quality is excellent.

DESIRED OUTCOMES

1. Streaming video – Enhanced ability for ailing members and out of town members to connect with Temple Shalom, religious services, and events taking place in our Sanctuary

2. iTemple – Enhanced ability of members to communicate with other members of the congregation, to find other members with similar interests, and to participate in committees and special groups.

3. Opportunities for intergenerational communication and connection.

4. Enhanced ability of individuals with a hearing impairment to participate in events taking place in our Sanctuary.

ONE FAMILY . . . MANY STORIES

About one and a half years into our One Family Initiative, we became aware of a new member who had participated in an interesting project in his previous congregation. He shared with us how the project worked. A small group of members of that congregation had been trained to lead one-on-one conversations with other members, focusing on the members' "stories."

It was easy to see the value of such a project for our Initiative; we developed a similar project, calling it **One Family . . . Many Stories**. Our new member, who brought this program to our attention, having a passion for this project, soon became the leader of this Action Group. The project was publicized in our monthly bulletin (Appendix 3E-1, p. 134).

We began, in several small group sessions, by training a cadre of volunteers to be Conversation Leaders. We developed an agenda for the training sessions (Appendix 3E-2, p. 135). We provided them with background materials (Appendix 3E-3, pp. 136-137) and a conversation guide (Appendix 3E-4, pp. 138-139) to help them get started. The Conversation Guide is just an aid to keeping the conversation going, not a list of questions that must be answered.

Over the next few months, we trained about fifteen volunteers who immediately arranged meetings with randomly selected Temple members and with new members. The conversations were to be limited to thirty minutes and could take place at Temple, a coffee shop, or anywhere comfortable for both parties. The conversations included their interests, concerns, passions, expectations, and their Jewish journeys. The information was collected and aided in connecting members to Temple activities and to other Temple members. It also provided information for the development of needed programs and affinity groups. The Conversation Leaders wrote brief reports about the conversations. The Action Group leader kept a database, and we watched for developing patterns.

An example of the type of outcomes this project can produce is our *Tikkun Olam* Council (TOC). One man who came to a training session participated in the role-play of a sample conversation. He was relatively new to our congregation and, during the process of the conversation, he shared a concern. He had participated in ongoing social justice experiences in previous congregations and had found nothing like that in this congregation. We did have some projects, but not the hands-on, ongoing experiences he had been used to. We realized that other conversation participants had made similar comments. This began a conversation among congregation leaders that ultimately led to the development of the *Tikkun Olam* Council, which would oversee the coordination of all existing social action/ social justice (*tikkun olam*) projects as well as identification and development of at least one ongoing project. (*Tikkun olam* refers to "repairing the world.")

After about six months, the interest of the Conversation Leaders waned, and these arranged conversations ceased. Faced with the possibility of losing this potentially valuable engagement tool, we met to brainstorm revitalization options. Three suggestions emerged, all providing more visibility for the project.

The first suggestion was to feature a member "story" in our monthly bulletin (after obtaining permission from the member). The second suggestion was to create an album of member stories to be kept available in our lobby or library and on iTemple (again, with permission of the member). The third suggestion was to recognize our Conversation Leaders, both in-person and in print.

We ran our first member story in the October 2016 bulletin. It did not result in any interest, and no more stories were presented. The other two suggestions did not take place. This project is on hold.

DESIRED OUTCOMES

1. Creation of new one-to-one connections among our members.

2. Identifications of members' interests, passions, and skills, and connection of members with similar interests, etc.

3. Identification of needed areas of programming for our congregation.

SHALOM CHAVERIM

About three and a half years into our transformation effort, we initiated our *Shalom Chaverim* (Welcome Friends) system, beginning with *Erev Shabbat* services and plans to expand over time to other events taking place in our Temple. Because we are a congregation dedicated to "audacious hospitality" (more about this in the next chapter) and to helping our members develop relationships, we established a plan for ensuring a friendlier environment for our members and guests. For *Erev Shabbat* services (and later, any special event taking place at Temple[1]) up to six team members (in addition to our two regular *Shabbat* Greeters[2]) welcome and assist attendees. The team members carry out very specific responsibilities. Beginning outside in front of our building, as people exit their cars and approach our front doors, two team members are there to welcome them and assist them

---

1) Because we have the largest Jewish venue in our community, other Jewish organizations use our facility for their events. When this happens, because attendees are guests in our Temple home, Temple members who are involved with that organization are asked to function as greeters.

2) For many years, this member couple has been functioning as *Erev Shabbat* Greeters. They are well acquainted with the congregation members and are likely to know who is and who is not a member. This on-going practice was not changed; they continue to carry out this function.

with walkers, wheelchairs, umbrellas, etc., as needed. As they enter the doors, our *Shabbat* Greeters wish attendees a *"Shabbat Shalom,"* give them our weekly handout and direct them to the appropriate next stop. **Members** are directed to the name badge cabinet where a team member is available to assist in finding their badges. **Guests** are directed to a table where a team member is waiting to assist them with guest badges. As attendees enter the sanctuary, two team members are available to help with seating and prayer books, especially helping guests and introducing them to someone sitting nearby. In addition, these team members assist individuals with special needs such as large print prayer books or amplification devices (loop system described earlier). At the *Oneg Shabbat,* all six team members are especially attentive to the guests, usually identifiable by their guest badges, making sure they are not sitting or standing alone.

To populate this plan with volunteers, we began by identifying one couple as Chairs of this Action Group. We then asked people we knew and some regular *Erev Shabbat* attendees to participate. Articles in our monthly bulletin invited the entire congregation to participate in this project (Appendix 3F-1, pp. 140-141). Each individual who agreed to participate is given an information booklet with a written description of this system, the Torah basis for providing this service, and a written description of the specific responsibilities (Appendix 3F-2, pp. 142-153). After trying an online sign-up platform (set up to enable the volunteers to identify which Friday evening they would be present and which role they wished to have), our *Shalom Chaverim* Chairs set up a less complicated email system for sign-ups. In addition, they sent weekly reminders to the *Shalom Chaverim* volunteers.

Besides engaging many of our members as team members (a worthy goal in itself!) and providing a very visible One Family project (also a worthy goal!), the goal of the *Shalom Chaverim* system is to ensure that everyone who enters our Temple home feels welcomed and valued. Every effort is made to provide a positive, friendly, experience for our members and our guests.

DESIRED OUTCOMES

1. Creation of additional experiences of a warm welcome for members and guests attending services and events in our Temple home.

2. Creation of visibility for our One Family Transformation when members and guests are in our facility.

3. Engagement of many members in a One Family experience.

OUR CONCIERGE

In addition to the above projects and changes, a part-time staff position was created to advance the Relational Judaism/One Family/Audacious Hospitality concept. This staff person is responsible for assisting members, new members, and guests in making connections, engaging in Temple life, and developing new relationships with other members and with Temple Shalom. This part-time position was added about one and a half years into the One Family Initiative and, after several iterations, is now called **Membership Engagement Coordinator and Concierge**. About one year later, as responsibilities increased and finances became available, this became a full-time staff position.

Because this person is responsible for greeting prospective members, a friendly, warm, and welcoming personality is a key requirement for this position. In this role, the Concierge has these responsibilities:

- Provide that all-important great first impression. The Concierge is often the first person callers and visitors encounter when contacting the Temple. She/he greets members and visitors as they enter the building during business hours. She/he responds to telephone inquiries, provides brief tours of our building, and answers questions. She/he makes sure people, members and prospective members, are directed to the appropriate staff person or volunteer leader.

- Participate in the planning of the One Family projects;

- Assist the leaders and volunteers, especially those associated with One Family or Membership, with each project as needed;

- Connect people with people and with activities that match their interests;

- Maintain a database of members' interests;

- Encourage involvement of members in congregational activities;

- Work with committees to promote involvement;

- Develop new initiatives to increase members' sense of belonging;

- Attend programs and services, as needed, to represent the Temple;

- Keep records regarding all who asked for information about membership, check back with them to answer questions they may have;

- Call members on their birthdays and anniversaries, providing well-wishes from the Temple.

Having a dedicated member on staff, connecting with people and dealing with the day-to-day matters at hand, relieves the rest of the staff from interrupting their work to respond to membership inquiries from phone callers and walk-in visitors. The Concierge not only has the time to do this, but it's his/her job! But, of even greater importance, **it makes a statement about how strongly we value people, relationships, and Audacious Hospitality.**

In the fourth year of our One Family Initiative, after the voluntary pledge system was initiated, our Concierge was so busy meeting with new and prospective members, it became necessary to hire a part-time person to answer the phone and respond to the doorbell.

ADDITIONAL *SHABBAT* SERVICE CHANGES

In addition to the name badges and our *Shalom Chaverim* system, Rabbi Miller has made some changes to the *Erev Shabbat* service that enhanced the welcoming atmosphere. This is important for this congregation. We have many visitors due to our location in a sunbelt resort community with an abundance of "snowbirds" and vacationers. We want these visitors and our members to feel welcome when they come to services whether they are "regulars" or not. We want everyone—members and guests—to have a positive, welcoming experience when they come to our Temple home.

At the beginning of the *Erev Shabbat* service, the Rabbi greets those who are watching the service on streaming video, our viewers in "internet land!" He then asks the congregation to rise and greet people around them. We warmly greet one another and introduce ourselves to guests, talk about where we are from (most of us are "from" somewhere!), engage in a little "Jewish geography" or just a friendly "How was your week?" In just these few minutes, an atmosphere of welcome and connectedness is created. When we settle back down to begin the service, our guests are no longer in a group of strangers but part of our "family."

In the middle of the service, soon after the *Mi Shebeirach* (prayer for healing), the Rabbi changes the direction and the tone, asking congregants to share the week's joyful events in their lives. He begins by reading the week's list of birthdays and anniversaries. Then we hear from our fellow attendees about each other's upcoming travels and homecomings, family *Bar/Bat Mitzvahs,* weddings, births, graduations, honors, visitors, travel experiences and new jobs. This is a warm, fun, and upbeat time in the service. All those who shared their joys are invited to the *Bimah* to participate in the *Kiddush* (blessing over the wine). Before they return to their seats, they are offered chocolate candies and encouraged to take handfuls to share the sweet experience with the rest of the congregation.

For many years, we have had a custom of introducing guests during the *Erev Shabbat* service. Expanding on that custom, the Rabbi asks guests to come forward to accompany the cantor in singing the Motzi (prayer over the bread) near the end of the service. Before the chanting begins, he asks their names and where they are from. This makes it easier for us all to see the guests shortly before we leave the sanctuary to go into the Social Hall, assisting members in identifying guests in order to welcome them.

Over time, the Rabbi's changes and One Family Team changes have transformed the ambiance of our *Erev Shabbat* experience. While the service had been upbeat and members enjoyed seeing one another before the changes, after the changes the atmosphere has become even more joyful and friendly. And we no longer hear from people who had visited or were "Temple shopping" that our *Oneg* was an unfriendly experience. Occasionally, if it has been a long time since their visit, someone we encounter in the community will say something about unfriendliness. Of course, we tell them how things have changed and invite them to come again. Living down a negative reputation can take a long time; people do not forget negative experiences. With our goal of "audacious hospitality" (more about this later), we have planned and worked diligently to create the warm welcome that will bring people back. Lest it sounds as if this welcome is mechanical or insincere, it is not. Even a brief greeting early in the service can lead to a longer conversation later at the *Oneg,* not only with guests but with other members we might not have known well. When these conversations happen, and common interests are discovered, relationships develop. And with every relationship, the connection to Temple is made stronger. Not only can this bring people back to Temple for services and events, it can also make the difference in the beginning or continuation of a membership!

SUMMARY

Each of the projects and changes that were a part of or related to our One Family Initiative has played an important role in our transformation to a relationship-based congregation. Even if the project didn't last, some new connections were made, and we learned from the experience. With each project, some new relationships developed, and our understanding of and dedication to the concept of focusing on relationships grew. When necessary, we made adjustments, found new leaders or volunteers or just moved on.

Some elements seemed to be common among the projects we undertook:

- We were not just developing programs but creating systems that facilitate the development of relationships and opportunities for engagement.

- Not everything worked out as we had planned. We needed to remain flexible and open to each other's ideas.

- Things moved slowly. Sometimes, in our zealousness, we set our expectations too high. We needed to be patient and realistic.

- Small groups are conducive to developing relationships.

- Programs and events often do better when they "bubble up" from the membership rather than decided upon by a group of leaders.

- Many of the changes we made, the systems we developed, or projects we undertook were built on existing Temple activities or structures or utilized existing committees.

- The joy is truly in the connections—the relationships—made with others and with the Temple.

While these specific projects—the ones presented in this chapter—were developed or advanced by the One Family Team to build relationships, One Family has come to mean so much more in Temple Shalom. One Family has come to refer to who we are and what we strive to be. Everything we do and the way we present ourselves to the larger community reflects the transformation that is taking place in the life of Temple Shalom. And make no mistake, change has—and is—taking place! The projects described in this chapter are the tools we have used to create our transformation, to become the One Family we want to be.

CHAPTER FOUR

SHARED VALUES – RELATIONAL JUDAISM AND AUDACIOUS HOSPITALITY

The Lord appeared to him by the terebinths of Mamre; he was sitting at the entrance of the tent as the day grew hot. Looking up, he saw three men standing near him, As soon as he saw them, he ran from the entrance of the tent to greet them and, bowing to the ground, he said, "My lords, if it please you, do not go on past your servant. Let a little water be brought; bathe your feet and recline under the tree. And let me fetch a morsel of bread that you may refresh yourselves; then go on—seeing that you have come your servant's way." They replied, "Do as you have said."

Abraham hastened into the tent to Sarah, and said, "Quick, three seahs of choice flour! Knead and make cakes!" Then Abraham ran to the herd, took a calf, tender and choice, gave it to a servant-boy, who hastened to prepare it. He took curds and milk and the calf that had been prepared and set these before them; and he waited on them under the tree as they ate.[1]

Genesis 18: 1-8, translation from TANAKH

THE CONCEPT AND THE SOURCE

My first encounter with the concept of Audacious Hospitality was in a presentation made by Rabbi Rick Jacobs, then President-elect of the URJ, at the 2011 Biennial Board meeting. At that meeting and others at the biennial, Rabbi Jacobs spoke of the need to "share Torah with all who search for its wisdom," "focusing on relationships over programs" and "removing barriers that have prevented people from finding their place in Judaism." He spoke of inclusion of all groups of people—interfaith families, interracial families, LBGT individuals and families, people with handicaps. Audacious Hospitality is described in URJ materials as being "about more than being a lovely host. It is being 'an organization that thinks outside the box' in order to allow people to participate and feel they are making a difference." Audacious Hospitality is described on the URJ website as

> "the focused effort to engage seekers in the sacred work of creating a world of wholeness, compassion and justice . . . [It is a] multi-faceted URJ initiative that encompasses some of our tradition's most treasured values—loving kindness, respect, and tikkun olam (repair of our world). It is all about putting the ideas of diversity, outreach, and inclusion into action—in a framework that addresses both today's Jewish communal needs and our highest aspirations."

Rabbi Jacobs and the URJ website put into words my feeling when I first encountered the concept of a relationship-based congregation in the mid-1990s. I was awed by what I heard then. I am thrilled now to be a part of a congregational attempt to live these values. In the URJ, we are taught to lead 'Jewishly,' to lead in *the way of Torah,* to bring *Torah* into our deliberations and decisions. The Torah quote at the beginning of this chapter provides guidance regarding the way we are to treat one another and "strangers." One cannot miss the sense of excitement, privilege, and personal involvement, which pervaded Abraham's acts of hospitality. No sooner had Abraham seen the travelers on the horizon that he ran to meet them from the entrance of his tent. He did not wait for them to approach him; he went beyond what was expected.

We, too, must go beyond the expected. We must be gracious hosts to all who come to our doors, all who seek to be a part of our community. And we must go beyond being gracious hosts. We must listen to our members, hear their stories, hear their expectations, hear their passions. We must meet them where they are, as Abraham met the travelers, and provide opportunities for the realization of their expectations and passions. We must help them connect with others who share their passions. We must provide the means for them to live their Jewish values and to explore their own spirituality.

Rabbi Jacobs emphasis on Audacious Hospitality continued at the 2015 Biennial, in Orlando, Florida. Our delegation, about fifteen of our leaders, returned from that assembly with great enthusiasm for the Audacious Hospitality concept.

As we continued our work with the One Family process at Temple Shalom, the words of Rabbi Jacobs came to mind. At Temple Shalom, we see Audacious Hospitality as the natural extension of Relational Judaism in our One Family Initiative. The relationship between Relational Judaism and Audacious Hospitality rings clear to us. At Temple Shalom, we see Audacious Hospitality as taking Relational Judaism to the next level, seeking to eliminate the barriers that prevent people and families from taking their place in our community and connecting with Judaism. To make Audacious Hospitality a reality at Temple Shalom, we must remove the barriers to membership and participation. We must be both gracious hosts **and** "think outside the box."

BEING GRACIOUS HOSTS

In the previous chapter, I shared a description of the ambiance experienced at our Temple's *Oneg Shabbat* of the past. I described how attendees tended to gather in groups of friends, sitting at round tables in "closed" circles, the result being what appeared to be an unfriendly environment—guests in a room of seemingly closed groups. Many of those who experienced such a negative introduction would be unlikely to return. An unfriendly *Oneg* experience is one barrier to joining or participating in a congregation. As I said earlier, change was needed. With our focus on values—relationships, member engagement, and audacious hospitality—changes were made. As described in Chapter Three, we developed our name badge system and our *Shalom Chaverim* project. Rabbi Miller made changes to the service that recognized and included our guests. He created a joyful atmosphere in the service.

Over time, these changes transformed the ambiance of our *Erev Shabbat* experience. While the service had long been up-beat and members had enjoyed seeing one another before to the changes, with the changes the atmosphere became even more joyful and friendly. No longer do we hear from people who were visiting or "Temple shopping" that the *Oneg* was an unfriendly experience. With our goal of "Audacious Hospitality" and our focus on relationships, we have planned and worked diligently to create the warm welcome that will bring people—guests and members—back to our Temple home. By doing this, we have removed one barrier to becoming a part of our community.

GOING BEYOND BEING GRACIOUS HOSTS

Just about everything we do as a One Family congregation is taking us toward Audacious Hospitality. Our efforts to provide engagement and connection among our congregants are directed toward being conducive to developing relationships, being inclusive. Our *Shalom Chaverim* system, changes in our *Erev Shabbat* service and the *Oneg*, our New Member Integration and *L'Shalom* (see Chapter Five) projects are in place to advance a sense of welcome into our community. The systems we have developed—name badges, affinity groups, our Tribute Garden, new member engagement activities, creating the position of Concierge, and more—connect our members with one another, not just at the entry level, but throughout the years of membership. Our projects have provided opportunities to listen to one another, to learn more about each other in small group settings. The addition of our Streaming Video and Hearing Loop, and the already available large print prayer books provide greater access and a more complete experience for shut-ins, members with hearing or vision impairment, and members who are unable to be here. Our redesigned Perman Library and our Tribute Garden provide spaces for small group conversation and connection.

When introducing the concept of Audacious Hospitality, Rabbi Jacobs spoke about removing barriers. One of the greatest barriers to joining a community—a community that could provide a means for expressing Jewish values, for educating Jewish children, for life-long education for adults, for developing the spiritual self—has been the requirement of paying dues to become a member. Indeed, as far back as I can remember the very definition of a member in a Jewish congregation has been one who pays dues. And to make the barrier even more difficult is the requirement to pay thousands of dollars into a building fund! Traditionally, in Jewish congregations, the "dues" has been a pre-set amount or amounts for various levels of membership (e.g., singles, families, young adults). Most congregations provide opportunities for relief upon request, some requiring documentation of need. This dues system can create a barrier to membership for those who, for whatever reason, cannot or do not want to pay the expected dues.

Many have described the process for requesting reduced dues to be "onerous" or humiliating, deciding not to join or to leave a congregation rather than asking for relief. Dealing with these barriers—dues and building fund—can be an enormous issue for any congregation. These barriers have been so pervasive in the Jewish community that there has been a sense they cannot be changed. A whole chapter, the next chapter, in this book has been devoted to addressing the issue of dues and building funds.

Another type of barrier is the member's own reluctance to "get involved." Many members will wait to be personally asked, and even then, the "ask" must interest them. It is up to us, the involved leaders, to reach out to them, to get to know their interests and passions, to provide many opportunities for involvement, many "doors"—appropriate doors—by which to enter. This is where listening becomes so important. Having a staff person, whose job it is to assist members in finding their door, their niche, is a great benefit in the engagement of our membership. At Temple Shalom, our Concierge is very helpful in connecting members with roles they might find fulfilling. Surmounting the barrier of reluctance can make all the difference for an uninvolved member, from drawing them in and to helping them feel they are contributing to the community in a meaningful way.

Relational Judaism and Audacious Hospitality share similar values, similar goals, and similar implementations. Both are processes toward congregational transformation from transactional program-centered thinking to relational thinking. Trying to separate them— Audacious Hospitality and Relational Judaism— is an unnecessary exercise in semantics. The important thing is to focus on the values and focus on the outcomes:

- a congregation that is welcoming and inclusive;

- a congregation that goes the extra steps to be inclusive;

- a congregation that knows the educational, spiritual, and social needs of its members because a means to listen is provided;

- a congregation that values relationships over programs or finances;

- a congregation that provides the means for the Jews in a community to explore Judaism and to live their Jewish values.

By maintaining this focus on values and desired outcomes when making policy decisions, developing programs, determining spending, and evaluating processes, a congregation is more likely to move towards becoming a relationship-based congregation.

CHAPTER FIVE

LIVING OUR VALUES – MATCHING FINANCIAL SUPPORT WITH RELATIONAL VALUES

The Lord spoke to Moses, saying: Tell the Israelite people to bring Me gifts; you shall accept gifts for Me from every person whose heart so moves him … And let them make Me a sanctuary that I may dwell among them.[1]

Exodus 25:1-2,8, translation from TANAKH

To fully embrace the values of Relational Judaism and Audacious Hospitality, we must consider and explore all aspects of Temple functioning—even our financial assumptions. Because the Temple's official relationship with the members begins when they join—that is, when they pay dues—even this interaction needs investigating. This chapter describes our examination of this "dues" interaction and where this investigation process led us.

OUR PROCESS

In March 2015, we were about one year into our One Family Initiative. A Temple Shalom Board member, with close ties to the Union for Reform Judaism (URJ), approached my husband, Neil, then President of our congregation, with information regarding alternative dues plans. Neil was interested in what he heard and did his own research into what was being called "voluntary dues systems" or "voluntary commitment systems." Neil read articles, rabbi's speeches, and URJ materials and he shared these materials with me. The information he collected intrigued him further. He formed a Dues Review Committee comprised of Board members, Finance Committee members, and other interested individuals (including me). He provided them with the background materials. The committee met and had discussions, considered whether or not a change was needed, whether or not some type of voluntary system would work for us, and just what system would be best for Temple Shalom. Thus began a two-year journey of learning, discussing, planning, and implementing for our lay leadership and staff.

In May of 2015, Neil attended a panel discussion in Newton, Massachusetts, led by Rabbi Dan Judson. The topic was "New Models of Synagogue Financing." The program, facilitated by a URJ leader (also a member of our congregation), was provided by the Combined Jewish Philanthropies of Boston and the URJ. Panel members were representatives of three synagogues that had implemented new models of financing. Neil came home with a sense that making this kind of change would be a meaningful step for our congregation. He believed it would be an important step in developing the cultural value-based change, the transformation, that the One Family Initiative was attempting to create at Temple Shalom. As Neil and I discussed changing to a voluntary system, we became aware of our growing sense that our traditional dues model (which we had never questioned before!) did not reflect the values of One Family. We became aware that the traditional dues system had been contributing to the creation of barriers to participation in a Jewish community. Furthermore, we came to understand that the traditional dues system is at the root of the transactional culture experienced by Jewish congregations. After all, the first **transaction** in the relationship that members have with the Temple is the **purchase** of their membership!

Shortly after returning from Massachusetts, Neil reported what he had learned to the Temple Board. Discussions continued through the summer of 2015 as Board members were provided with materials and information. Materials included:

Chernov, B.P., Joseph, D. & Judson, D. (2015). Are voluntary dues right for your synagogue: A practical guide? Synergy: Innovations and Strategies for Synagogues of Tomorrow (Vol. 8).

Glassman, M. (7/6/2015). Temple changes to voluntary dues structure. Florida Jewish Journal/Broward Jewish News. **www. sun-sentinel.com/florida-jewish-journal/news/broward/fl-**

jjbs-dues-0708-20150706-story.html

Judson, D. (1/12/2012). Scrapping synagogue dues: A case study. http://ejewishphilanthropy.com/scrapping-synagugue-dues-a-case-study/

Materials from Temple Beth El, Aptos, CA. www.tbeaptos.org

Materials from Temple Emanu-El, Marblehead, MA. www.emanu-el.org

Re-Envisioning Engagement: Re-Imagining Congregation Membership and Dues Models. Reform Jewish Outreach of Boston.

In the fall, a few members of our Dues Review Committee developed demographic and financial information of our congregation regarding:

- Ages of members, those who joined and those who resigned;

- Donations of members and non-members;

- Donations to our on-going supplemental fundraising over a three-year period;

- How much was collected over a three-year period;

- How many members were on dues relief and how much they paid collectively.

In January 2016, a meeting was held for Board members, the Dues Review Committee members, Finance Committee members, and staff. A speaker—the executive director of a temple that had successfully made the change from a dues system to a pledge system—was brought in to further the discussion of alternative commitment systems. The speaker described her congregation's process, which took six months and shared their materials (letters to members, etc.). Having this speaker present and available provided our leaders with the opportunity to ask questions and to develop a better understanding of the reasons for a change. They learned some variations of a voluntary system that had been used and processes that would increase the chances of success.

Over the next several months, the Dues Review Committee collected data and materials from other congregations that had adopted some form of voluntary commitment system. What did their process look like? How did they present the concept to their members? What letters did they send their members? Did they provide FAQs? Did they prepare "elevator" speeches?

Mostly for my own use, I compiled a set of pros and cons, congregational impacts, preparations for implementation, and change options—a summary of the information gleaned from the readings. This summary is presented in Appendix 5A, pp. 154-159.

By June of that year, the Board was ready to take the decision process to the next step. The Dues Review Committee was expanded, forming the Commitment Committee. This Committee represented a cross-section of the Temple population including Board members, religious school parents, preschool parents, Finance Committee members, senior citizens and our Executive Director. This Committee discussed, brainstormed and considered options. Neil, Finance Committee members, and our Executive Director collected more data regarding non-paying members (honorary members, life members). They developed an analysis of the cost to run the Temple per adult member, the result then being called the "sustaining amount."

In August 2016, after a review and discussion of materials and analyses, the Committee unanimously approved changing to a voluntary pledge system and agreed to take the proposal to the Temple Executive Committee. The Executive Committee also approved the change and agreed to take the proposal to the Temple Board. The change to a pledge system was unanimously approved by the Board. With a plan in mind to begin using our new pledge system for the 2017-2018 fiscal year, Neil and the Executive Director developed a timeline for our process. This timeline is available in Appendix 5B (pp. 160-161). While we were not able to follow the dates on the timeline, we did (loosely) follow the steps that were planned.

OUR RATIONALE for CHANGE

In the *Book of Exodus*, we read how our Israelite ancestors brought gifts **as their hearts moved them** to provide for the construction of the *Mishkan*, the Tabernacle (see quote at beginning of this chapter). Every gift, no matter the size, was considered worthy and was valued. As we so often find, *Torah* is providing the guiding concepts. Being true to the teachings of *Torah*, an important rationale for changing the way our members financially support the Temple, is the creation of consistency between the values we espouse and the way we actually do things. As a congregation committed to *Torah* and Relational Judaism—our One Family Initiative—we are committed to the values of relationships, equality, respect, connections, welcoming and inclusion. As we are reminded by the value statement of Audacious Hospitality, we believe in the necessity to remove barriers to membership and participation. We believe our expectation of financial commitment and support from our members should reflect these values. The traditional dues system does **not** do this. The negative effects of the traditional dues system include:

- The humiliation inherent in the need to **request** relief if an individual or family feels they cannot afford the "standard" amount, speaking with the Executive Director and producing income tax forms to verify income (the latter practice had been discontinued in our congregation some years earlier);

- The possibility that those who pay less than the standard dues might feel their membership is somehow of lesser status, possibly resulting in reduced participation;

- The barrier that the dues system (and the building fund) could create for prospective members;

- The need for staff and lay leaders to act in the role of bill collectors;

- The transactional nature of the dues system (purchasing a membership!), fostering a fee-for-service mindset.

As we learned the negative effects of our traditional dues system, we came to understand this change in the way our members financially support our *"mishkan"* was needed. It became clear to us that the traditional system was not reflective of our Jewish and relational values or who we were striving to be. Basic among our values is our belief that every Jew has the right to a religious experience regardless of their ability to pay. By definition, the standard dues system and the building fund create a group of members who, due to an inability to pay these fees, become that segment of our Temple family that must go through the onerous process of requesting relief. Other values such as focusing on people's needs, inclusion, connecting and engaging and our desire to be a sacred community, also demand a system that respects our members, their interests, and passions, as well as their financial differences.

A "voluntary" pledge system eliminates these barriers to membership and participation because the individual or family establishes their own level of commitment with no oversight by a representative of the Temple. Our *"L'Shalom"* (For Temple Shalom) system, the name we gave our new system, allows each member unit to set a level of giving that works for them, **as their hearts move them**. There is no need to justify or verify the level of giving. In addition, all members are considered equal, regardless of their ability to pay. There are no longer categories of membership. The *L'Shalom* system is in keeping with the values of our One Family Initiative by including all who want to be a part of our One Family, by respecting our members' sensibilities and by reducing the financial barriers to membership and participation.

IMPLEMENTATION OF OUR *L'SHALOM* PLAN

The next step in our change process was to take the plan to the members of the congregation. Because we had done a great deal of research regarding the need for careful presentation to the members—clarity regarding the reasons for the change, a clear description of what the change is and how it will affect them—the Board delegated this step to the Marketing and Communications Committee. Before the end of August 2016, the Marketing Committee began meeting to deal with this change and the general marketing needs of the Temple. The work of the Marketing and Communications Committee relating to One Family and the change from a standard dues system to a pledge system continued into January 2017. Details are described in Chapter Six.

Our presentation of the change to the congregation began in January 2017. Following the plan set out by the Marketing and Communications Committee, a letter explaining the *L'Shalom* Pledge System was sent to every member that month. A second letter and pledge cards were mailed to the congregation in March 2017. By the end of June (the end of our fiscal year), over ninety percent of the members' pledge cards had been returned. Those who had not returned their pledge cards received "gentle reminder" phone calls from selected staff and lay leaders. As of July 1, over eighty percent of our congregants previously known as "seasonal affiliates" became full and equal members of the congregation. Also, before the beginning of the new fiscal year, thirty-seven new members (units) had signed pledge cards, commiting to join the congregation. Other outcomes of the *L'Shalom* pledge system are discussed in Chapter Seven. By November 2017, there was a sense of positivism—joy, success, "we did it!" While we knew more time was needed to know if the change had been successful, we did believe the change had furthered the transformation from a transactional (fee for service) culture to a relational value-based culture.

The concept of Relational Judaism includes fostering members' connections with members, members' connections with Temple, with Torah, and with God. Most of our One Family Initiative efforts prior to introducing *L'Shalom* had focused on relationships among members. The change to a voluntary pledge system adds a focus of the relationship of members with Temple. With this change, we feel we are demonstrating our values and living our Judaism as communicated by God to Moses for building God's tabernacle. The practice of accepting "gifts of the heart" has long been the norm by other faiths. **By eliminating the standard dues system and the building fund, we are removing major barriers to membership and participation, making it possible for more of our co-religionists in our community to have a synagogue connection.** We have demonstrated respect for our members by removing the onerous need to **request** a dues reduction when circumstances require it ("hat in hand," as the expression says). We are living Relational Judaism and Audacious Hospitality!

CHAPTER SIX

SHARING THE VISION – AGAIN AND AGAIN

"When the seventh month arrived—the Israelites being [settled] in their towns—the entire people assembled as one man in the square before the Water Gate, and they asked Ezra the scribe to bring the scroll of the teaching of Moses with which the Lord had charged Israel. On the first day of the seventh month, Ezra the priest brought the Teaching before the congregation, men and women and all who could listen with understanding. He read from it, facing the square before the Water Gate, from the first light until midday, to the men and the women and those who could understand; the ears of all the people were given to the scroll of the Teaching.

Ezra the scribe stood upon a wooden tower made for the purpose . . . Ezrah opened the scroll in the sight of all the people, for he was above the people; as he opened it, all the people stood up. Ezra blessed the Lord, the great God, and all the people answered. "Amen, Amen," with hands upraised. Then they bowed their heads, and prostrated themselves before the Lord with their faces to the ground. Jeshua, Bani, Sherebiah, Jamin, Akkub, Shabbethai, Hodiah, Maaseiah, Kelita, Azariah, Jozabad, Hanan, Peliah, and the Levites explained the Teaching of God, translating it and giving the sense; so they understood the reading.[1]

Nehemiah 8: 1-8, translation from TANAKH

THE EARLY DAYS OF THE ONE FAMILY INITIATIVE

For the first two and a half years of the One Family Initiative, I prepared many of the One Family communications with the congregation, usually getting input from Neil and our co-chair before they were submitted to our Director of Communications. These communications included:

- Emails to the members of the One Family Team

- Bulletin articles describing the projects and inviting participation. (See sample articles in Appendices 2G, pp. 106-108, and 6A, p. 162.)

- During the High Holiday season, 2014, we had large posters in the Temple lobby (Appendix 6B, p. 163) complete with photos related to the activities we had operating at that time.

- A glossy, trifold brochure prepared for High Holydays 2015, describing our Initiative and our projects (Appendix 6C, pp. 164-165). This brochure was available on a table in the Temple Lobby for about one and a half years.

- A report for the annual meetings in the spring, outlining our activities to date (Appendix 6D, pp. 166-167).

- A page linked to our Temple website (Appendix 6E, pp. 168-174).

In addition to the above communications, some Action Group leaders wrote bulletin articles regarding their projects and some prepared small blurbs for the *Erev Shabbat* handout (examples in Appendices 3A-1, p. 111, and 3C, p. 130). We all made many phones calls—the direct "ask" is still the most likely way to engage people.

Because we wanted the support and involvement from as many of the lay leaders and staff as possible, over time Neil and I contacted individuals and groups to request their participation and, sometimes, to request financial support. We met with the leaders of Sisterhood and Men's Club. We had prepared a handout for them about the projects we were working on at that time (Appendix 6F, p. 175). Neil and our Co-Chair reported regularly to the Board. We met with the Rabbi occasionally to ensure that we were on the "same page." I met with the Director of Education and the Preschool Director. We worked with the Facilities Manager on some projects. At one time or another, for one project or another, most of the lay leaders and staff were involved in the One Family Initiative.

After writing lengthy, periodic bulletin articles for two years, several people advised me that congregants are not likely to read so much material. For the next year, I submitted two one-liners each month (Appendix 6G, pp. 176-177) for publication in the monthly bulletin. These one-liners were brief statements describing One Family, what it is and what we do, followed with direction to the One Family information on the Temple website. I hoped that these brief statements would stimulate interest and perhaps inquiries. After a year, having had no response, I discontinued the one-liners in the monthly bulletin and sought help from the Marketing and Communications Committee. They liked the one-liners and suggested continuing them. They also suggested occasional short paragraphs, also in boxes, in the monthly bulletins.

MARKETING AND COMMUNICATIONS COMMITTEE

In August of 2016, I joined the newly reorganized Marketing and Communications Committee. The first task we undertook was the writing of a new mission statement for Temple Shalom. Several meetings were devoted to this task. After several iterations, we agreed on the following wording:

> Temple Shalom of Naples is an inclusive Reform congregation where all individuals are equal partners in making our world whole and holy. We are One Family, believing in the sacredness of relationships, fostering connections—one to another, Temple, Israel, Torah, and God. We are living Jewish values and nurturing future generations.

This statement was submitted to the Temple Board and was approved. This new mission statement now appears in the Temple Board Room and in the Temple Lobby and is prominently placed weekly in our *Shabbat* handout and monthly in our Temple bulletin. It appears sporadically in other publications as is appropriate.

You can imagine my delight that a statement so focused on One Family values would come to be the central statement of who we are and what we do. After only two and a half years of the One Family Initiative, the central values of One Family had become those recognized by the congregation leadership and shared with the congregation and community!

Another task undertaken by the Marketing and Communications Committee that summer was the development of a new Temple logo. We had already begun using the tag line—One Family, Many Connections. We wanted a logo that would work with this tag line. A professional graphic designer was brought in to help us. She came to a Committee meeting and asked questions about our values and our symbols. She took pictures of various iconic features in the Temple. At the next meeting, she presented some designs; these did not meet the expectations of the Committee. Again, she listened to the wishes and concerns of the Committee. She returned with the "hands" concept now in use. After some finetuning regarding colors, fonts, and placement, the logo was finalized (Appendix 6H, p. 178). It was presented to the Board and it was approved.

This logo is unique to Temple Shalom. It was presented to the congregation in January 2017 issue of our monthly bulletin with an explanation of the symbolism (also in Appendix 6H). This logo is inherently and uniquely descriptive of Temple Shalom and representative of the Temple Shalom tag line—One Family, many connections.

Again, this logo with its focus on One Family places the values of our Initiative front and center whenever it is used. The Marketing Committee expects that this logo will become synonymous with Temple Shalom.

DEMONSTRATING ONE FAMILY VALUES FINANCIALLY

With our new mission statement and logo in place, the Marketing and Communications Committee directed attention to the *L'Shalom* pledge system (Chapter Five). Having learned from multiple sources the importance of the initial introduction to the congregation, we reviewed the processes and materials of other congregations that had transitioned from a dues system to a pledge system. We understood the importance of the wording of the letter. We borrowed ideas from various sources. In a process of writing and editing by a few members of the Committee, submitting the letter to the Committee as a whole for further editing, and repeating these steps, we created a letter to send to the congregation. We tested the letter with a focus group, collecting their comments and making changes based on their concerns. We repeated the writing and editing process, producing a final form of the letter (Appendix 6I, pp. 179-180). This letter was mailed to each member household. It is important to note that this letter, and all those that followed, emphasized that this change was value driven, that the change was being made to bring our practices in line with the values we espoused!

We presented the Torah quote, the one that begins Chapter Five, as a reference to our Torah values.

A set of FAQs was posted on the Temple website (Appendix 6J, pp. 181-183). In order to provide opportunities for our members to ask questions and express concerns, four dates for "town hall" style meetings were arranged, and this information was included in the first letter. These meetings were held, and a total of about thirty members attended. In March, another letter and accompanying pledge form (both in Appendix 6K, pp. 184-185) were mailed to all members. We asked that the pledge cards be returned by April 30. A reminder with a new deadline was mailed early in May and reminders appeared in our monthly bulletin, our weekly e-blast, and our *Erev Shabbat* handout (Appendix 6L, p. 186). By June 30, all but about forty pledge cards had been returned. Some of our members included checks with their pledge cards, even though this was not required.

We had expected that some pledge cards would not be returned and planned for specific staff members and the president of the congregation to make phone calls. This was done with good results.

Our process regarding the *L'Shalom* pledge system was the result of a great deal of research and planning, beginning with reading the materials from other congregations, then determining who would write our materials, to developing our materials, through introducing the *L'Shalom* pledge system to our members. Our Marketing and Communications Committee was comprised of individuals with skills in writing, marketing, and/or knowledge of the One Family Initiative and the *L'Shalom* pledge system. Our Director of Communications is also a part of this committee.

The success or failure of changing from a dues system to a pledge system depends greatly on the initial presentation to the congregation. Each congregation is different. For us, the Marketing and Communications Committee felt that aligning the support system with Torah values and our One Family values would be the most meaningful. As you will see in our letters to the congregation, this was our approach (Appendices 6I and 6K). After explaining the planned change, we also provided access to more information to read and opportunities to attend gatherings where they could ask questions.

The marketing strategy of the One Family concept and the *L'Shalom* pledge system reflects the concept presented in the Text quote at the beginning of this chapter. The repetition of the name and the concept in many settings and many times, the connection to our values, and the careful wording of our communications are in line with the care that Ezra and his aides took to explain the "Teaching of

God" in a way that the people would understand the reading—that they would have "a mind to understand," "eyes to see," and "ears to hear."[2]

The launching of our *L'Shalom* pledge system went well. We were glad we took the time and effort to prepare our materials carefully. In February 2018, the Marketing and Communications Committee met to begin development of a letter and pledge card for the second year of *L'Shalom* (Appendix 6M, pp. 187-189).

CHAPTER SEVEN

EVALUATION – WHERE WE WERE AND WHERE WE ARE

God said, "See, I give you every seed-bearing plant that is upon all the earth, and every tree that has seed-bearing fruit; they shall be yours for food. And to all the animals on land, and to all the birds of the sky, and to everything that creeps on earth in which there is the breath of life, [I give] all the green plants for food." And it was so. And God saw all that he had made, and found it very good. And there was evening and there was morning, the sixth day.[1]

Genesis 1: 29-31, translation from TANAKH

SOME BASICS OF EVALUATION

The basic word in program evaluation is *change*. The big question for non-profit organizations is *did this program result in change*—change in people's lives, change in knowledge, change in attitudes, change in statistics, change in something? Sometimes these changes are easily expressed quantitatively (for example—number of members) and sometimes they are more abstract, more conceptual (such as attitudes or opinions). Change is usually expressed in more or less of something—increases or decreases. To determine if that increase or decrease has taken place, you must know the level of the "something" in question before it was influenced by the program in question. This is your *baseline*.

When gathering baseline information, it is helpful to plan evaluation before one begins a program, to consider the types of changes one desires to achieve and to gather that data before embarking on the program at hand. Some data can be recreated after the fact—such as membership numbers or donation dollars at a given time. But some information is more elusive such as attitudes or levels of satisfaction at a given time. One cannot recreate this information at a later date. One can only speculate based on a sense of things, or extrapolate from related quantitative data. If levels of donations have increased, that may be an indication that the level of satisfaction has increased. Or it may be a reflection of an improvement in the economy. Yet, even if we do not have the baseline information we would like to have, if we are to lead Jewishly (see Torah quote above), we must follow the example established by God in the Biblical story of creation. We must periodically look at what we have done and evaluate our work.

EVALUATING A CONGREGATIONAL PROGRAM

Levels of satisfaction among the members of a congregation can be a very elusive concept. Surveys of one kind or another (mail, email, or phone) are the instrument usually employed to gather this information. The value of a congregational survey depends on knowing what questions to ask and how to ask them, knowing the **indicators** of satisfaction. Some of these indicators may be common to most congregations, and some may differ depending on the congregation's religious affiliation, history, size, competition, and location in the community and in the country. Frequently, congregation leaders, both lay and professional, will object to surveys. Sometimes, when evaluating satisfaction, the best one can do is get a "feel" for how the congregation is regarded by the members. Is there a sense of joy, of camaraderie, of being together? Is there a lot of grousing in conversations regarding the congregation? Is there a pride in membership or talk of leaving the congregation? What kinds of things are being said about the congregation by members and by non-members?

In some cases, membership numbers can be indicative of a level of satisfaction. If the congregation is growing, this could be a sign that the level of satisfaction is increasing. Or, it could mean that there is a change in community demographics (for example, the Jewish population of the area is increasing). If the congregation is declining in membership, this could be an indication that there is a decrease in the level of satisfaction. However, the decrease may again be related to community demographics (the size of the Jewish community is declining or there is increased competition in the area). Or the changes in congregation size could be related to internal changes in membership policies and have less to do with satisfaction.

EVALUATING THE ONE FAMILY INITIATIVE AND THE *L'SHALOM* PLEDGE SYSTEM

When we were starting our One Family Initiative, the One Family Team brainstorming elicited some "measurable" desired outcomes of our One Family efforts:

- Increased participation in the life of Temple Shalom;
- Increase in positive talk about the Temple;
- Increase in hits to the Temple website;
- Increase in membership;
- Increase in donations to specific projects;
- Improved financial stability.

As it turned out, the first three of these outcomes were not so measurable at Temple Shalom. Because, at the time the outcomes list was compiled, we hoped that we could do a congregational survey. We had expected to have baseline data regarding these outcomes. However, due to an earlier survey and earlier advice from outside consultants, the survey prior to introducing Relational Judaism and a later one requested prior to introducing the pledge system (a second "baseline" survey) were not approved by the congregation leaders. Without those surveys, we do not have baseline data for these outcomes. Therefore, we cannot empirically determine if there was a change in satisfaction levels, participation levels, or hits to our Temple website. We can only extrapolate from the data we do have.

Regarding the remaining three outcomes listed, while none are relational, we do have data leading to these conclusions:

Membership: In the first three years since we introduced Relational Judaism, our One Family Initiative, there was a small yearly rise in membership. After introducing our L'Shalom pledge system, there was a large increase in membership numbers! It appears that removing the barriers of a dues system and a building fund is attractive to those considering membership! Furthermore, in the years since introducing One Family, very few members left the congregation due to dissatisfaction (zero to two per year). The net result is a growing congregation!

Donations to Special Projects: When we began the One Family it was understood that every project needing funding must find donors to cover their expenses. Because there was no money budgeted for our projects, this expectation became part of the One Family culture. For example, as we began our first project, name badges for every adult member of the congregation, members stepped forward to provide either the funds or the materials to make the project happen. For some projects, our Sisterhood and Men's Club have provided funds. For some projects, we have recruited funders in our monthly bulletin. For some projects, members have stepped forward on their own to provide funding. We are so grateful to those who have provided this financial support for our One Family projects!

Financial Stability: In the years since we began the One Family Initiative, Temple Shalom has ended each fiscal year "in the black." Even after changing from a dues system to a self-determined pledge system (see Chapter Five), we met our financial goals with annual commitment pledges exceeding the amount budgeted. Contributing to this positive end of year financial position was the One Family culture of funding our projects and to careful and controlled spending by the congregation leadership.

Interviews with Knowledgeable Individuals: In order to get a better sense of the change that had taken place, I interviewed our Rabbi Emeritus of Temple Shalom, our cantor, and our current president. The Rabbi Emeritus served as Senior Rabbi for fifteen years prior to and immediately before Rabbi Miller and is still very active in our congregation. Our Cantor came to Temple Shalom in 2010 and works closely with Bar/Bat Mitzvah students and their families. Our current president has been a congregation leader for many years.

As I had hoped, the Rabbi Emeritus shared his perspective of Temple Shalom as it was prior to the beginning of our One Family Initiative. He described the culture of Temple Shalom as transactional in nature, but with relational factors already in place. The congregation was a "fertile field" for a relational initiative. While the congregation was demographically fragmented (very little mixing of the generations of members), Temple Shalom served as the "Jewish community" for many of the Jews of Naples. Jews lived in many different communities throughout the greater Naples area, then and now. There was no one part of the area that could be designated as being Jewish (as was often the case in midwestern cities), making Temple Shalom their "Jewish address." He described Temple Shalom as a resilient congregation with many good people serving in leadership. He said "conditions were ripe" for these leaders to look ahead and be open to new ideas. These factors laid the groundwork for a transformational initiative. As the Rabbi Emeritus described it, One Family was "not created from nothing." What One Family did was to "sharpen the focus" of Temple Shalom's relational direction.

The Cantor described Temple Shalom as being a welcoming congregation even before we began our One Family Initiative. However, with the Initiative in place, the welcoming nature became a "more conscious effort" resulting in an even more welcoming congregation. She shared her perspective regarding One Family and possible future activities. This information will be very helpful going forward!

A conversation with our current president resulted in a description of our congregation as being "already in a good place" before One Family. She said it was a "good time to attempt refining our focus."

As you can see, all three of these leaders describe a healthy congregation before we began One Family, an organization healthy enough to be open to new ideas and new ways of doing things.

These are all positive results—the membership numbers, the donations to special projects, the financial stability, and the impressions of our leaders – all contributing to our One Family sense of success. The real changes are the opportunities for engagement for our members—the "people connecting with people" changes —and the "people connecting with Temple" changes. Beginning with our name badges and our at home *Shabbat* Dinners, with our streaming video and our loop system, to our newest *Shalom Chaverim* greeters, new ways to connect and engage have occurred. The joy with which we greet each other on *Shabbat* and at other Temple activities is apparent. The concerted efforts to ensure that guests feel welcomed—whether by our *Shalom Chaverim* greeters on *Shabbat* or by our Concierge when they stop by Temple to check us out—has surely played a role in the increase in membership. The feelings of inclusion and engagement likely have contributed to the members' willingness to be financial supporters of our One Family projects. I believe it is fair to say that our One Family projects have played a role in transforming our beloved Temple Shalom into a relational, value-based congregation. The One Family Initiative paved the way for our *L'Shalom* pledge system, refocusing our mindset on our values. Our values-based and Torah-based *L'Shalom* pledge system is very much a part of this transformation, removing barriers to membership and participation. With the impact of these additions and changes and the Rabbi's modifications to our *Shabbat* service, we can "feel" the transformation taking place. We are becoming the relational, value-based congregation we strive to be.

OTHER INFLUENCES ON OUTCOMES

Many factors enter into changes in outcome data. While it may appear that the changes that occurred in Temple Shalom's data regarding the outcomes described here are **causally** related to the One Family Initiative and to the change to the pledge system (this is to say, that the One Family Initiative and the *L'Shalom* Pledge System **caused** the changes from one time to the next), other factors may also contribute to these outcomes. Congregations do not exist in a vacuum; internal and external factors change and may influence the outcomes. Some of these factors could be:

- Stability in the clergy staff;

- Continuing support of the clergy, support staff, and lay leaders;

- Presence of the Membership Concierge who focuses on membership development and involvement (this internal change is part of the One Family Initiative;

- The makeup and influence of the board and the finance committee and their leadership;

- The careful and deliberate efforts of the Marketing and Communications Committee in communicating with the congregation and the general community;

- The growing Jewish community in Southwest Florida;

- Improvement in the local and national economy.

While it is important to recognize that there are factors other than the two major changes (One Family Initiative and the *L'Shalom* Pledge System) influencing the outcomes, these two changes were major events in the life of Temple Shalom. The changes were surely strong influencers on the outcomes we used as evaluators.

CHAPTER EIGHT

GOING FORWARD – LIVING OUR ONE FAMILY VALUES

Rabbi Tarfon used to say, "You are not required to complete the work, but neither are you at liberty to abstain from it."[1]

Pirke Avot: 2.21, translation appears in Gates of Prayer

WALKING THE WALK

In Chapter One, I wrote about congregations depending on members as a resource, both financially and as a labor force. It makes sense for a resource that important to be the focus of thinking and action when a transformational process is under way. Relational Judaism and voluntary pledging certainly move us in that direction. Developing the relationships—the connections of members to each other and members to the Temple—contributes to a sense of ownership among those members that is basic to a healthy organization. But as some would say "You can't just talk the talk. You have to walk the walk." We began "walking the walk" by finding ways to respond to the members' needs, passions, and interests and proactively engaging the members in Temple life—a key factor of a Relational Judaism transformation. In our process, we listened to the ideas that were priorities for our Team members and implemented those ideas. Some projects worked for a while, with interest diminishing over time, ultimately fizzling out. Some projects worked from the beginning and continue to assist our members in making connections. We continue to look for ways to enhance those connections, ways that strengthen their ties to each other and to Temple. We look for ways to demonstrate how much we value our members. And every time we strengthen those relationships, we are "walking the walk" of Relational Judaism.

Another major factor in creating a relational transformation is **financially** demonstrating the value of the members, 1) making the way we spend money reflect the importance of the members and 2) making the way we support the Temple reflect our respect for the members. Our first step in this direction was the creation of a staff position focused on engaging the members and welcoming visitors. Hiring our Concierge (Membership Engagement Coordinator), demonstrates that we will spend money to have a staff person whose job it is to help the members get involved! Again, we are "walking the walk."

Our next financial step toward our relational transformation—and it was a big step!—was the shift from a standard dues system to a pledge system. We communicated that this change was being implemented to bring our practices— even our financial practices—in line with our values of respect, of equality, and of Torah. With a carefully planned introduction of this change, the members responded well. The very positive response to the pledge system, besides being financially advantageous for members and for Temple, is symptomatic of a change in the right direction and "walking the walk."

With this change to a pledge system, we also discontinued having various levels of membership demonstrating our values of equality and respect among our members. The category of Seasonal Affiliate (the designation given to "snowbirds" who wanted to be a part of a congregation while they were here; not a membership level) was discontinued, granting full and equal membership to all who pledged an amount of their choosing. Over eighty percent of those who had previously been Seasonal Affiliates sent in their pledge cards by the end of our first fiscal year using our *L'Shalom* pledge system.

In addition to the reception of our new *L'Shalom* pledge system by the members of our congregation, it appears that members of the community are learning about the "new" Temple Shalom. The rate of membership increase rose a great deal more than it had in previous years. It appears that "putting our money where our mouth is" was well received by our congregation and by our community. "Walking the walk" communicates sincerity; members and others recognize sincerity and respond to it.

ONE FAMILY – THEN AND NOW

Before we began our One Family Initiative, Temple Shalom was a wonderful congregation with a great religious school, an award winning preschool, strong adult education programs, an active Sisterhood and Men's Club, many functioning committees, and recurring events. Then and now there was and is an active cadre of volunteers.

When the One Family Initiative began introducing our projects—name badges, *Shabbat* Dinners, One Family-Many Stories, etc.—they felt like "add-ons" to the regular programs of the congregation. The One Family projects felt somehow "separate." As time passed and as . . .

- Rabbi Miller and the lay leaders referred to Temple Shalom as One Family;

- Board members included their "passions" in their weekly comments from the *Bimah* at *Shabbat* services;

- Our new tag line, new mission statement, and new logo became visible in our monthly bulletin, our letterhead, our Shabbat handout, and other Temple publications;

- Rabbi Miller included the One Family concept in his sermons, especially on the High Holidays;

- The *L'Shalom* pledge system became an accepted way of doing things;

. . . the One Family concept expanded and encompassed our sense of who we are. In the beginning, we talked only in terms of a One Family Initiative. Now we can refer to our process as a transformation because we can see the change that is taking place. The ambiance at services and the *Oneg* on Friday evening, the response from members when the word goes out that donations are needed for a specific project, the response from members and community to the *L'Shalom* pledge system—all are symptomatic of the change that is happening. One Family and the values it represents have become an integral part of the Temple Shalom identity and experience. Temple Shalom continues to be a vibrant congregation!

WHAT IF...

It is important to note that it is possible this initiative/transformation might not have taken place (at least not in its current form) had Rabbi Miller not attended that CCAR meeting in 2013 where he learned about Relational Judaism. His Relational Judaism vision for Temple Shalom might never have developed. Had I not attended the URJ Regional Biennial in the 1990s, I might never have known about the relationship-based congregation pilot project happening in my region. I might never have been inspired to share the idea with Rabbi Miller. In 2015, fifteen members of our Temple Shalom leadership attended the North American Biennial in Orlando, Florida. For those fifteen members, their understanding of Audacious Hospitality and their enthusiasm and motivation to further the development of the concept at Temple Shalom were immensely increased by their experiences at that convention. What if Neil, as president of the congregation, had not been open to change and had not attended the 2015 conference in Boston where he gained an understanding of the value of a voluntary pledge system. These types of gatherings—the CCAR meeting, the Regional Biennial, the North American Biennial, and conferences—are examples of opportunities for growth and development for congregation leaders. Gatherings that bring our Reform Jewish community and its leaders together provide information about what other congregations are doing and what the scholars of our time are teaching. **What if** Rabbi Miller and our congregation leaders had not attended these meetings? Taking advantage of these learning opportunities provides leadership development, programming ideas, management solutions, and lead to an understanding that we, the individual congregations, are a part of a much larger whole, and so much more. Congregations would do well to not only encourage their leaders, lay and professional, to attend as many of these meetings as possible but should also subsidize their attendance. The congregation will benefit from the knowledge gained and enthusiasm engendered!

GOING FORWARD

By no means are we finished. There is still work to be done. As the quote from Pirke Avot at the beginning of this chapter indicates, we are obligated to continue this work. Each generation of members, each generation of leaders, must undertake the tasks at hand, and move us to the next level. As God's partners on earth, we must continue the tasks of making the world a better place. Here at Temple Shalom, besides supporting our still young *Shalom Chaverim* project, we are looking into:

- *Developing new Havurot (friendship groups)* – Some of the *havurah* (singular) groups that were started two decades ago are still in existence. Others have disbanded. Most *havurot* (plural) are comprised of twenty members or less and meet in members' homes or other designated small-group venues. Under the leadership of a past president and our Concierge, we recently brought together the members of the congregation interested in such groups. These leaders created an invitation, application form, and cover letter (Appendix 8A, pp. 190-192) and a *Havurah* Handbook (Appendix 8B, pp. 193-205). The havurah concept is explained in detail in this Handbook. A meeting was held in April 2018, with about sixty people in attendance. The agenda for this meeting is in Appendix 8C (p. 206). The process of creation of new *havurot* has begun and, as of this writing, ten groups have formed!

- *Creation of Affinity Groups* – These groups, based mostly on demographics, would not be limited in size and would be open to any member who fits the parameters of the group. One group, Empty Nesters, got started and had some gatherings a few years ago. Interest has waned in the last year. We would like to revive this group and start others. We have had several requests for an Interfaith Families group and are currently in the planning process for such a group.

- *New Member Mentors* – The third major planned addition to our new member welcoming is *B'ruchim Habaim* (welcome), a mentoring program. The plan is for each new member individual or family to be assigned to an individual or family who will mentor them throughout the first year. Every effort will be made to ensure a good match, taking into consideration the demographics and interests of the mentees and the mentors. The mentors will be asked to invite the mentees to attend services and events with them and to get together with their mentees at least once away from Temple. The purpose of this aspect of our welcoming plan is to ensure that coming to services or events during their first year feels comfortable and friendly and again, to develop new relationships.

- Fine-tuning various Temple programs, committees, and projects, in concert with their leaders and participants, to determine if there are relational systems that would serve them. The One Family Initiative is an ongoing process; reviewing and fine-tuning keep the concept current and fresh.

- Seeking to identify demographic groups that may be underserved by our One Family projects. Have we left anyone out? What relational systems would be meaningful to them?

OUR RELATIONAL TRANSFORMATION PROCESS IN REVIEW

Undertaking a process that will require the involvement of many members and take years to accomplish should have outcomes that are worthy of the effort.

The outcomes of a relationship-based congregational transformation include:

- a membership that is connected, engaged, and dedicated to the synagogue or church,

- a membership that is unlikely to leave due to dissatisfaction,

- membership numbers that are growing, attracting new members from the community.

If members of the congregation are content and membership numbers are growing, there is a possibility for financial stability (assuming there is responsible financial management as well!).

Sharing our transformation process and helping other congregations get started is really the point of this book. With that in mind, here is a summary of our basic concepts and the steps we took:

1. **Determine the congregation's readiness** to begin a process of transformation. Review the best-practices checklist and address those areas where improvement is needed.

2. **Ascertain the support of professional and lay leadership.** Before beginning a transformational process, leaders must buy into the need for change and the direction of the process.

3. **Identify the congregation's values** in a collaborative process with the board. Discuss the importance of including these values in decision making.

4. **Select a Team of volunteers** to help get the process started. This Team should expand beyond board members and be representative (at least loosely) of the demographics of the membership.

5. **Provide an attention-getting event for the whole congregation** to begin sharing the vison of a relationship-based congregation. Provide information about the value for the congregation.

6. **Expand the Team of interested members** by inviting all members of the congregation to participate.

7. **Hold meetings with the Team and the Board** to:
    a. Choose a name for the process;

b. Continue educating Team and Board members with workshops;

c. Brainstorm ideas focusing on projects that promote interaction among the congregation members, ideas that are doable in the near future and ideas that have enthusiastic supporters;

d. Prioritize ideas on the basis of doability, impact, and passionate leadership for each activity;

e. Identify enthusiastic leaders and group members for each project; help them get started, making sure that they share your vision for their project; (Do not let chairs fall into the "it's easier to do it myself" trap. The idea is to include and engage as many people as possible.)

f. Determine funding issues.

8. **Periodically review what is working and what is not;**

a. Determine which projects are working well, which can be salvaged, and which need to be discontinued; focus on the quality of the experience rather than the number of participants;

b. Add new ideas over time based on the same criteria. Do not try to start too many new things at one time (three to four seems to work initially, adding one or two at a time after that).

9. **Include and engage as many congregation leaders (professional and lay) as possible.** Take the time to meet with staff members, educators, sisterhood and brotherhood leadership, and committee chairs. Assure them you are not invading their work but would like to include them and those they represent in your projects. Listen to their ideas for your process.

10. **Communicate with the congregation** in as many ways as possible—monthly bulletin, blast email, Sabbath service handout, in sermons and announcements, website, and annual reports. Use the chosen name of the process as often as possible to promote familiarity;

11. **Include relational values and the name of the process in the congregation's mission statement, logo and letterhead.** Hopefully, over time, the name of your relational process and the name of your institution will become synonymous for your membership and in your community.

12. **Share your congregation's ideas with others.**

There is no way that one person can make all these things happen. It takes a team effort with a great deal of support from the congregation's leaders—staff, board, and chairs. There is no room for being territorial in this process. The three words that are key to this process are INCLUDE, LISTEN, and ENGAGE. Moving together toward the same goal, this is an "eye on the prize" effort. And from what I have seen in my congregation, it is well worth it!

A LOOK TO THE FUTURE

We will continue adding projects and fine-tuning existing projects as we move forward. Please follow our updates on current and new projects on our website **drtussyshnider.com/blog.** I hope by sharing our experiences, this book and the updates are helpful to other congregations.

REFERENCES

Introduction

1. **www.seniorliving.org/leisure/pathway-to-longevity/** Power of Relationships and Pathways to Longevity

Chapter One

1. *TANAKH: The Holy Scriptures,* (Philadelphia: The Jewish Publication Society, 1985), p. 321.

2. D. T. Shnider, "Management Factors Associated with Perceived Effectiveness in Reform Jewish Congregations: Questionnaires Eliciting Leader and Member Perspectives," *Dissertation Abstracts International, OCLC WorldCat,* The Ohio State University, 2002.

3. S. P. Robbins, *Organizational Behavior: Concepts, Controversies, and Applications,* (Englewood Cliffs, NJ: Prentice Hall, 1990), p. 725.

4. R. N. Anthony and D.W. Young, *Management Control in Nonprofit Organizations (5th ed.),* (Boston: Irwin, 1994), p. 47.

5. P. F. Drucker, Managing the Nonprofit Organization: Principles and Practices, (New York: HarperCollins, 1990), p. xiv.

6. Anthony and Young, op. cit., p. 72.

7. M. Harris, "The Power of Boards in Service Providing Agencies: Three Models," Administration in Social Work, 18(2), pp.5-6.

8. Anthony and Young, op. cit., p. 72.

9. Shnider, op. cit., pp. 20-21.

10. D. P. Forbes, "Measuring the Unmeasurable: Empirical Studies of Nonprofit Organization Effectiveness from 1977 to 1997," *Nonprofit and Voluntary Sector Quarterly,* 1998, 27, pp. 185-186.

11. R. D. Herman and D. O. Renz, "Nonprofit Organizational Effectiveness: Contrasts between Especially Effective and Less Effective Organizations," *Nonprofit Measurement and Leadership,* 1998, 9, p. 26.

12. R. D. Herman, D.O. Renz, and R. D. Heimovics, "Board Practices and Board Effectiveness in Local Nonprofit Organizations," *Nonprofit Measurement and Leadership,* 1997, 7, p. 375.

13. Shnider, op. cit., p. 46.

14. Ibid., p. 47.

15. Ibid., p. 33.

16. Ibid., p. 108.

17. Ibid., p. 47.

18. Ibid., pp. 47-48.

19. M. Gibelman, S. R. Gelman, and D. Pollack, "The Credibility of Nonprofit Boards: A View from the 1990's and Beyond," *Administration in Social Work,* 1997, 21(2), p. 31.

20. Ibid., p. 32.

21. Shnider, op. cit., p. 109.

22. Gibelman, Gelman, and Pollack, op. cit., p. 36.

23. T. P. Holland, D. Leslie, and D. Holzhalb, "Culture and Change in Nonprofit Boards," *Nonprofit Measurement and Leadership,* 1993, 4, pp. 148-149.

24. Ibid., pp. 147-148.

25. Harris, op. cit., p. 5.

26. Ibid., p. 8.

27. R. F. Leduc and S. R. Block, "Conjoint Directorship: Clarifying Management Roles between the Board of Directors and the Executive Director," *Journal of Voluntary Action Research,* 1985, 14(4), p. 72.

28. J. Pfeffer, *Managing with Power: Politics and Influence in Organizations,* (Boston: Harvard Business School Press, 1992), p. 247.

29. Ibid., p. 258.

30. Ibid., p. 260.

31. D. B. McGaw, "Commitment and Religious Community: Comparison of a Charismatic and a Mainline Congregation," Journal for the Scientific Study of Religion, 1979, 18, p. 157.

32. Harris, op. cit.

33. P. A. Zelanski, C. E. Zech, and D. R. Hoge, "Determinates of Religious Giving in Urban Presbyterian Congregations," Review of Religious Research, 1994, 36,

34. Shnider, op. cit., p. 111.

35. Ibid., p. 112.

36. Cited in W. A. Chess and J. M. Norlin, *Human Behavior and the Social Environment: A Social Systems Model (2nd ed.)*, (Boston: Allyn and Bacon, 1991), p. 51.

37. Ibid., p. 49.

38. Ibid., p. 134.

39. Ibid., p. 133.

40. Ibid., p. 134.

41. W. G. Plaut, *The Torah: A Modern Commentary*, (New York: The Union of American Hebrew Congregations, 1981), pp. 1537-1538.

42. Ibid., p. 1537.

43. Ibid., p. 1535.

44. Ibid., p. 782.

45. *Tanakh: The Holy Scriptures*, (Philadelphia: The Jewish Publication Society, 1988), p. 1519.

46. Ibid.

47. Drucker, op. cit., p. 158.

48. Ibid., p. 37.

49. Ibid., p. 44.

50. F. Hesselbein, The Effective Organization, *Executive-Educator*, 1992, 14(3), p. A17.

Chapter Two

1. *TANAKH: The Holy Scriptures,* (Philadelphia: The Jewish Publication Society, 1985), p. 113.

2. S. Sinek, *Start with Why: How Great Leaders Inspire Everyone to Take Action* (NY: Portfolio/Penguin, 2011), p. 20.

Chapter Three

1. *TANAKH: The Holy Scriptures,* (Philadelphia: The Jewish Publication Society, 1985), p. 224.

Chapter Four

1. *TANAKH: The Holy Scriptures,* (Philadelphia: The Jewish Publication Society, 1985), p. 25.

Chapter Five

1. *TANAKH: The Holy Scriptures,* (Philadelphia: The Jewish Publication Society, 1985), p. 123.

Chapter Six

1. *TANAKH: The Holy Scriptures,* (Philadelphia: The Jewish Publication Society, 1985), p. 1519.

2. Plaut p. 1537.

Chapter Seven

1. *TANAKH: The Holy Scriptures,* (Philadelphia: The Jewish Publication Society, 1985), p. 4.

Chapter Eight

1. *Gates of Prayer: The New Union Prayerbook,* (New York: Central Conference of American Rabbis, 1975), p. 20.

APPENDIX 1A

Relational Judaism Initiative – Organizational Readiness Checklist

The items on this checklist are suggestions based on organizational research, organizational experience, and Torah teachings. It is suggested that your board members be asked to respond individually to the items listed followed by a collective tabulation and discussion regarding each item.

It is not expected that all items be checked off as being done by your congregation to be ready to begin a Relational Judaism initiative. However, because these behaviors have been shown to be associated with effective functioning, the more items to which your leaders can honestly respond positively, the more likely your congregation is ready to be introduced to a new way of thinking and doing things. Those items to which there is a consensus of negative responses can be worked on simultaneously with your Relational Judaism initiative.

SHARED VISION

Behaviors	Yes	Maybe/ Sometimes/ Not sure	No
1. The board of my congregation has engaged in the process of identifying the core values of the congregation.			
2. The board of my congregation has established a written mission statement for the congregation.			
3. The mission statement for my congregation was developed in a collaborative effort by leaders of the congregation.			
4. Jewish values are included in the mission statement for the congregation.			
5. My congregation's mission statement appears on various publications, notices, brochures, or mailings.			

APPENDIX 1A: Relational Judaism Initiative –
Organizational Readiness Checklist

SHARED VISION *(cont'd.)*

Behaviors	Yes	Maybe/ Sometimes/ Not sure	No
6. The stated mission of the congregation is considered in decision making by the board.			
7. The board of my congregation has established long-term goals for the congregation.			
8. The board of my congregation has established short-term goals for the congregation.			
9. The board of my congregation has developed a time-line for the achievement of long-term goals.			
10. The established goals are considered in decision making by the board of my congregation.			
12. The board of my congregation periodically reviews the mission for the congregation.			
13. The board of my congregation periodically reviews the goals for the congregation.			

BOARD DEVELOPMENT

Behaviors	Yes	Maybe/ Sometimes/ Not sure	No
14. The board of my congregation puts time and effort into board education.			
15. An annual board orientation program is provided for members of the board of my congregation.			

APPENDIX 1A: Relational Judaism Initiative –
Organizational Readiness Checklist

BOARD DEVELOPMENT *(cont'd.)*

Behaviors	Yes	Maybe/ Sometimes/ Not sure	No
16. The board of my congregation engages in ongoing board training experiences. (Examples include such activities as retreats, field trips, and mini-lessons at board meetings.)			
17. The board of my congregation participates in opportunities for education and leadership training offered by the Union for Reform Judaism. (Examples include sending a delegation to the biennial conventions and attending visits by URJ representatives.)			
18. I am aware of my congregation's long-term goals.			
19. I am aware of my congregation's short-term goals.			
20. As a member of the board, I was supplied with a "board notebook" containing information such as the by-laws and policies of my congregation, a board roster, congregational history, staff roster, etc.			
21. The board of my congregation focuses on policies of the congregation rather than the day-to-day operation of the temple.			
22. The board of my congregation considers the process for dealing with issues to be as important as the substance of the issues.			
23. The board of my congregation routinely engages in Torah study at our meetings.			

BOARD DEVELOPMENT *(cont'd.)*

Behaviors	Yes	Maybe/ Sometimes/ Not sure	No
24. When making decisions, the board of my congregation includes lessons from Jewish texts in the process of determining the best conclusion.			
25. In my congregation, participation by board members and others in URJ leadership is encouraged.			

SELF-EVALUATION

Behaviors	Yes	Maybe/ Sometimes/ Not sure	No
26. The project planners engage in a formal evaluation of the event when such events are completed.			
27. After a congregational event or program, members of my congregation are asked for their opinions regarding that event or program.			
28. Our board periodically evaluates the performance of programs and projects regarding mission and goals of the congregation.			
29. When evaluating programs or projects, the board includes Jewish values as a part of its review process.			
30. Our board has a prescribed practice for evaluating the process by which decisions are made and issues resolved.			

APPENDIX 1A: Relational Judaism Initiative – Organizational Readiness Checklist

SELF-EVALUATION *(cont'd.)*

Behaviors	Yes	Maybe/ Sometimes/ Not sure	No
30. Our board has a prescribed practice for evaluating the process by which decisions are made and issues resolved.			
31. The board of my congregation periodically measures progress toward the achievement of the congregation's goals.			
32. The board of my congregation evaluates its performance in some recurring and systematic manner.			

MEMBER EMPOWERMENT

Behaviors	Yes	Maybe/ Sometimes/ Not sure	No
33. The views of my congregation's members are sought and included in board deliberations.			
34. Our congregants are informed regarding issues that will be deliberated at upcoming board meetings.			
35. Our congregants are informed regarding decisions made at board meetings.			
36. Our board meetings are open to members of the congregation.			
37. Members of the congregation are encouraged to attend board meetings.			

APPENDIX 1A: Relational Judaism Initiative –
Organizational Readiness Checklist

MEMBER EMPOWERMENT *(cont'd.)*

Behaviors	Yes	Maybe/ Sometimes/ Not sure	No
38. The leaders of my congregation are approachable and easily accessible.			
39. I feel valued and appreciated as a volunteer worker in my congregation.			
40. In my congregation, volunteer service is appreciated and recognized as demonstrated in multiple ways such as a mention in the monthly bulletin, public recognition event, personal notes, advancement in the organization, etc.			
41. In my congregation, members who put forth time and effort in volunteer activities have access to leadership positions, even the presidency.			
42. In my congregation, I feel comfortable making suggestions regarding issues and programs even if my ideas differ greatly from past procedure.			
43. It is easy to become involved in the life of my congregation, to participate in programs, projects, and/or committee work.			
44. Leadership training opportunities are available to all interested members of the congregation.			
45. The nominating process for leadership is delineated in our congregation's documents.			
46. The nomination process delineated in our congregation's documents is followed.			

MEMBER EMPOWERMENT *(cont'd.)*

Behaviors	Yes	Maybe/ Sometimes/ Not sure	No
47. The process for nominating leaders in my congregation allows input from the membership.			
48. As a member of the board, I can make good decisions because I have adequate information about the issues.			
49. As a board member, I am encouraged to ask questions regarding issues on which I will be voting.			
50. When board members are considering an issue, alternative perspectives are examined.			
51. The diversity of opinion is welcomed and respected in my congregation.			
52. Committee chairs are encouraged to develop committees to carry out the committee's function.			
53. In my congregation, the responsibilities of the clergy, staff, and board are well delineated.			
54. The by-laws delineate a succession plan regarding the position of president.			
55. The succession plan regarding the position of president is generally followed.			

APPENDIX 1B

Ten Conditions for Motivating Volunteers

1. **Provide a sense of belonging**

   Help each volunteer feel he or she is a valued member of the group. Provide on-going training. Build a structure in which volunteers have opportunities for small group participation and interaction. Make sure information is widely shared and readily accessible.

2. **Provide role models**

   Encourage interaction between the organization's leaders and other volunteers. Encourage volunteers to participate in organization activities. Take every opportunity to bring leaders from regional and national levels and other organizations to work with your volunteers. Encourage attendance at regional and national meetings and conventions.

3. **Engender a sense of achievement**

   Use every opportunity to recognize the work of members, both in writing and orally—newsletters, local newspapers, at meetings, and events. Say thank you in many ways and as often as possible. Recognize achievers by promotion to higher positions, promoting those individuals who have demonstrated commitment and responsibility.

4. **Insure an environment that is focused, fair, and fun**

   Focus on the tasks at hand, not on personalities or money. Make sure everyone has an opportunity to contribute to discussions and be respectful of people's feelings. Create an "up" mood, sharing your enthusiasm for the work of your organization!

5. **Encourage curiosity and creativity**

   Encourage members to ask why things are done and why things are not done. Value the member that questions the status quo. Encourage varying points of view in a discussion. Be careful not to belittle any contribution to discussions.

6. Encourage a spirit of adventure

Be willing to try new things and new ways of doing old things. If the new way doesn't work, try another new way. Don't get "stuck in a rut"! Be willing to take risks; never assume a new idea is impossible.

7. Develop a sense of leadership and responsibility

Each volunteer should have specific responsibilities. Give volunteers opportunities to express their ideas and make decisions. Encourage involvement in various organization activities and at meetings.

8. Build confidence

Be generous with praise. Find something good about each participant's contribution to the group effort. Provide supervision for volunteers, guiding their work, but do not re-do the work they've done.

9. Provide a sense of purpose

Stay focused on your mission and values. Begin each meeting or project with an educational experience that is value-based. Re-evaluate your mission statement regularly and insure that all volunteers see it frequently. Make your mission a part of your decision-making process.

10. Provide a sense of direction

Engage in long-range planning. Establish long- and short-range goals and strategies to achieve those goals. Discuss the mission and goals with the volunteers as they engage in their assigned tasks.

Adapted from *Motivating Your Child: Eight Conditions That Make a Difference* by Quaglia & Cox, University of Maine as seen on Today, NBC, 8/16/98

Developed by
D. Tussy Shnider, Ph.D.
The Shnider Group
1998, rev. 2004

APPENDIX 2A

Wolfson's Twelve Principles

TWELVE PRINCIPLES OF RELATIONAL ENGAGEMENT

As per Dr. Ron Wolfson

1. PERSONAL ENCOUNTERS: **Creating opportunities** for members to build relationships with each other and for staff and lay leaders to build relationships with our members.

2. TELLING STORIES: **Encourage others to talk** about who they are, where they're from, what they value, their Jewish journey, what they hope for in our congregation; **sharing our own stories**. **Actively listening** to what others have to say.

3. LEARNING TOGETHER, DOING TOGETHER: Studying, socializing, doing mitzvot as **part of a group**. Developing study partners, celebrating Shabbat together.

4. CONNECTING: **Caring about each other** in times of sadness and times of joy; engaging with people we don't know; emphasizing what we have in common; helping people connect to Temple life.

5. EXPERIENCES: Sharing content and emotion, food and participation, action and celebration can be just as important as the program. **Doing things that require interaction**, extending experiences beyond the Temple walls.

6. VOLUNTEERISM: Asking members to identify and share their talents, abilities, and passions and to respond to a personal appeal to **get involved as partners on a team**. Use language that reflects team participation. Focus on activities with meaning to the members—reflecting mitzvot and the ethical base of Reform Judaism.

7. FOLLOW-UP: Asking is the first step of engagement but the second step is to **sustain the relationship** by further contact.

8. TRANSITION POINTS: From institution shopper to member, from preschool to religious school, from Bar/Bat Mitzvah to high school, from high school to college, from post-college to young Jewish adulthood, and from child-rearing to empty-nesting—**assisting people at the transition times in their lives.**

9. RE-ENGAGEMENT: **Reaching out to those who were involved before** and encouraging them to get involved again, giving them a new sense of connection.

10. RELATIONAL SPACE: **Enhancing the Temple environment** to aid in relationship building; **taking Temple life and Judaism outside of the building** to homes and community.

11. RELATIONSHIP MEMBERSHIP MODELS: **Enhancing a culture of belonging** to a community in which people care for and learn about each other, network with and teach each other, and give back to the community; **reaching out to meet the needs of various demographic groups**.

12. RELATIONAL LEADERSHIP: Taking the time to **create opportunities to build relationships** and work together, vertically and horizontally, even if it isn't the easiest or most expedient way to get things done; **empowering others**; training leaders.

Developed by Tussy Shnider, Ph.D. and Neil Shnider, MBA, CPA
Temple Shalom, Naples, FL
December 2013

APPENDIX 2B

The Shabbat Shalom[a] –
Introducing Relational Judaism at Temple Shalom

October 18, 2013

TEMPLE SHALOM AND RELATIONAL JUDAISM

As the Rabbi indicated on the High Holidays, Temple Shalom, with the support of the Board of Trustees, has embarked on the implementation of "Relational Judaism". This program has received national attention and is being developed throughout the country by Union of Reform Judaism (URJ) Temples. Relational Judaism refers to a shift in emphasis in congregation life, focusing on the relationships among the people involved, with each other, with the community, with Torah, and with Jewish values. We are delighted to participate in the growth and enrichment of Temple Shalom and to be part of this exciting endeavor. It is important that we have a good cross-section of members of the congregation as part of our team. Please think about the opportunity of being at the forefront of this congregation-wide initiative and join our team in this important part of Temple Shalom's growth.

Please send us an email.

We will be having a meeting in the next few weeks.

L'shalom

November 15, 2013

ONE FAMILY – RELATIONAL JUDAISM AT TEMPLE SHALOM

What role does Temple Shalom play in our lives?
What do we want for ourselves, our families, our community?
The synagogue has long been known as a house of prayer, a house of study, and a house of gathering. What does this mean to us?
Our Relational Judaism Team is focused on engaging our members in relationships
With other members
With learning
With Mitzvot
With Torah
With God

We need your input. We need your involvement.
Help shape the future of Temple Shalom!

---

a. *The Shabbat Shalom* is a handout provided for all attendees of the weekly Shabbat service. It includes a program of the service, articles about upcoming events and other materials. Article(s) reproduced with permission of the author(s) and the Temple Shalom Executive Director.

APPENDIX 2C

D'var Torah – First Team Meeting

Parashat Chaye Sarah
Gen 23:1 – 25:18

The *Parashat* for this week is *Chaye Sarah*. One theme in this *Parashat* is Abraham's dispatching of his trusted servant to find a wife for his son Isaac. The servant traveled to Abraham's native land, chose Rebekah to be Isaac's wife, and they and their entourage traveled to the Land of Israel where Isaac takes her for his wife. In this story, the hospitality toward Isaac's servant demonstrated by Rebekah and Laban, her brother, is described in detail. That hospitality is, indeed, instrumental in the choosing of Rebekah to be Isaac's wife. Rebekah and Laban understood the needs of the strangers and attended to them. This follows the pattern of the previous *Parashat* in which Abaraham's hospitality to three strangers is also described.

Hospitality to strangers is a recurring theme in Torah. The theme of hospitality provides us with a guide to behaving Jewishly toward the strangers among us. Here, at Temple Shalom, one obvious group of "strangers" would be our prospective members, those whom we have never met. Perhaps even some of our current members, those with whom we have little or no relationship, are strangers among us as well. In Torah and in our prayer books, we are reminded that we were once "strangers in a strange land" and are frequently admonished to welcome them. Here, in Naples, many of us came as strangers, were new in town, in the not-so-distant past. Surely, here, we, of all people, understand that the strangers among us must be welcomed, be heard, be included, be drawn-in.

- May we be guided by Torah, by the examples of Abraham, Rebekah, and Laban, to hear and to heed the needs of others.

- May we build relationships with our "strangers."

- May we, in the work we embark on this morning, find new ways to listen, to be welcoming, to include, to draw-in, to build new relationships and deepen existing ones.

Keyn Yehi Ratzon – May this be God's will.

APPENDIX 2D

First Team Meeting – Agenda

Relational Congregation Team Meeting
October 27, 2013
Agenda

1. Welcome

2. Purpose of our Team – Our Charge
   How we will meet this challenge?

3. D'var Torah

4. Introductions – Please be brief!

   a. Name

   b. Why did you join Temple Shalom?

   c. Think back to your first involvement at Temple Shalom. How did that involvement come about?

   d. What do you expect to accomplish in this team effort?

5. What we will do – Our first steps

   a. Immediate changes we can make? – brainstorming

   b. Where do we begin? – prioritizing

6. Identifying roles for team members

7. Identifying who will do what

8. Set date for next meeting

APPENDIX 2E

Desired Outcomes for First Meeting

Relational Congregation Team
First Meeting
Outcomes & Activities

1. **Increase in understanding of Relational Judaism**

   a. Ask participants to read Wolfson book before meeting

   b. Discuss twelve principles and identify some things that could be different at Temple Shalom.

   c. Discuss outcomes for Relational Congregation experience.

2. **Greater sense of relationship among team members**

   a. Tell stories including

      i. Aspirations for participation in Temple life

      ii. Skills and interests

   b. "Listen hard"—active listening; take notes

   c. Discuss why team members want to be involved in this experience

3. **Determination of early steps of our process—where do we begin**

   a. Discuss ideas for immediate changes (e.g., seating in lobby, volunteers in office)

   b. Interviews – work on interview guide

4. **Identification of roles for team members (based on information developed in #3)**

5. **Select date for next meeting**

Article in *The Voice*[b] for Opening Event

January 2014

SAVE THE DATE!

**DR. RON WOLFSON
AND "RELATIONAL JUDAISM"
COMING TO TEMPLE SHALOM**

On February 2, 2014, Dr. Ron Wolfson, author of *Relational Judaism: Using the Power of Relationships to Transform the Jewish Community*, will be the keynote speaker at Temple Shalom's One Family kick-off lunch.

Congregations across North America are recognizing the need to make a cultural shift in their approach to meeting the needs of their members. A growing awareness of societal and environmental changes – changes in family configurations, changes in expectations, and changes in the way we communicate—require new responses in temple functioning. Dr. Wolfson maintains if a temple is to remain relevant in the lives of its members, a focus on the expressed needs and interests of the members and facilitation of relationships of members with each other, with Torah, and with Judaism is needed.

Dr. Wolfson's book provides insights into what it means to be a relational congregation and the principles involved. On February 2 he will share with us the excitement this approach is creating in the Reform Jewish world. As Dr. Wolfson states in his book, "The purpose of a synagogue is to be a sacred community of people whose lives are enriched with meaning, purpose, connectedness, and a relationship with God through prayer, study, acts of social justice, healing, and lovingkindness...our goal is . . . to transform membership into a covenantal relationship between the individual and the spiritual community . . . "

Please join us on February 2 as we become one of the congregations to take this meaningful and enriching step into the future!

---

b. *The Voice* is the monthly publication of Temple Shalom mailed to all members of Temple Shalom. Article(s) reproduced with permission of the author(s) and the Temple Shalom Executive Director.

Article in *The Voice*[b] – Opening Event

December 2013

SAVE THE DATE
TEMPLE SHALOM'S ONE FAMILY
KICK-OFF EVENT
FEBRUARY 2, 2014 at 11:00 A.M.

Keynote Speaker: Dr. Ron Wolfson
author of
Relational Judaism: Using the Power of Relationships
to Transform the Jewish Community

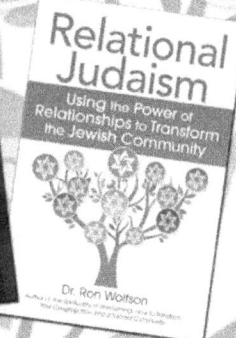

The entire Temple Shalom Family is invited to a Presentation at 11 a.m. with Lunch to follow.
Together we will learn to understand the covenant of relationships
between individuals and the spiritual community.

Dr. Wolfson will also have a book signing, so bring your book!
Books will be available for purchase.

DO NOT MISS
THIS OPPORTUNITY TO
HELP SHAPE THE FUTURE
OF TEMPLE SHALOM!

Please call the Temple Office to rsvp.

APPENDIX 2G

The Voice[b] **Article**

December 2013

One Family –
Relational Judaism at Temple Shalom

Our Relational Judaism Team is focused on engaging our members in relationships

- With other members
- With learning
- With Mitzvot
- With Torah
- With God

Our plan is to develop both global and small group activities. This is an initiative that involves the entire Temple membership. Relationship building has always been a part of congregational life in the committees and organizations that are part of our Temple family. We must learn from those experiences to help the efforts of the One Family initiative.

Over 30 members attended the first meeting held at the Temple. After telling about their own expectations, the Team members had an informative discussion about some relationship-building activities. Team attendees volunteered for actions that will get us started and add to the connections among our members.

It is important to engage a vast variety of demographics and talents in this transformational effort. With the involvement and participation of many age and interests groups, many backgrounds and expectations, we can better understand the stories of our members and help them connect.

We need your input. We need your involvement.

Help shape the future of Temple Shalom!

The Voice[b] Article

June 2014

One Family News

Our Temple Shalom One Family initiative has been enthusiastically engaged in developing various processes for congregation members to connect with one another. Six Action Groups have been formed and are in various stages of organizing. The Action Groups and their areas of focus are as follows:

Ambassadors – The focus of this group is to establish a group of volunteers who will welcome visitors, develop processes to integrate new members, dialogue with new, current, and exiting members, and develop avenues that will draw members to participate as members of our Temple family. The existing Membership Committee will be an important part of this Action Group.

***Shabbat* Dinner Action Group** – The focus of this Group is to organize a series of *Shabbat* Dinner and *Havdalah* events of various sizes, configurations, and locations. The events will provide opportunities for our members to share the *Shabbat* or *Havdalah* experience with other members of our Temple family in settings that encourage the development of relationships.

One Family Home Action Group – This Group is focusing on our Temple facility, identifying and exploring ways our building can be more conducive to welcoming visitors to Temple and more conducive to relationship development.

Affinity Groups Action Group – This group is charged with the development of various interest groups based on demographic, professional, and other areas of similarity. This effort is being developed using the "empty nesters" as a model affinity group.

Communications/Technology Action Group – This Group is updating the Temple database and developing social media venues for Temple.

Intergenerational Activities – This Action Group is still in the formation stage. Several people have expressed interest in working with others who wish to develop opportunities for our congregants of varying generations to work together

Our One Family Team has met periodically to develop these plans, establish goals and time-lines, and review and coordinate what each of the Action Groups is doing. The Action Groups are fluid and evolving – new groups can and will be added as needed. Participation is open to all who are interested in being a part of this Temple transformation.

WE WELCOME YOUR INVOLVEMENT!!

If you would like to be part of this exciting initiative, please contact us or the Action Group leaders.

Relational Judaism Workshop

One Family Steering Team Meeting with
Temple Shalom Board of Trustees
December 17, 2013
Agenda

1. D'var Torah

2. Introduction

3. Discussion: WHY?
   - Why change?
   - Why now?
   - Why Relational Judaism?

4. Relational experience:
   - Break into random small groups
   - Find out what the members of the group have in common. (five minutes)
   - Share results.

5. Discussion: WHAT and HOW?
   - Present Ron Wolfson's twelve principles. (handout)
   - Assign principles to the groups for discussion and expansion, answering these questions:
     + What activities could be done to exemplify/advance the principle?
     + How would these activities be the same as or differ from what we are already doing?
     + Do we have to change behaviors to accomplish this principle and, if so, how?
     + Is this a feasible activity or change?
   - Share and discuss results

6. Communicating with the congregation: More HOW?
   - Developing an "elevator speech"
     + Each group write a brief statement (no more than 30 seconds long)
     + Share results
   - Eight ways to greet a stranger in the synagogue (handout)

7. Prepare for Ron Wolfson's presentation:
   - What questions do we want to ask him?
   - Request volunteers for February 2 event

APPENDIX 3A-1

The Voice[b] **Article – *Shabbat* Home Dinners**

August 2014

SHABBAT HOME DINNERS
OFF TO A GREAT START IN JUNE!

Three dozen Temple members have enjoyed a wonderful Shabbat dinner and we want to share their excitement with you. Here are some comments:

"Last evening was so wonderful and warm, and we thank you for including us in your ONE FAMILY initiative home dinner."

"It was a fantastic evening!!!!!!!!!"

"What a lovely and relaxing and delicious Shabbat! You had a special evening of wonderful conversation with congregants that have now become good friends."

More dinners are scheduled for this Summer.

If you would like to be a guest at a future Temple Shalom Home dinner or possibly host one please contact:

APPENDIX 3A-2

Article in *The Shabbat Shalom*[a] – Shabbat Home Dinners

May 9, 2014

One Family Shabbat Dinners

June 13 and June 27

In keeping with the One Family initiative, some of our congregants have graciously volunteered to host Shabbat dinners in their homes and provide a main dish.

APPENDIX 3A-3

One Family *Shabbat* Dinner
Phone Invitation Script

- Hi, this is _____. How are you?

- I am a member of Temple Shalom and I am hosting a Shabbat Dinner at my home as part of our One Family Initiative.

- I would like you to join me/us at my/our home for Shabbat Dinner on _____.

- If yes...Wonderful! I will be making the main course. I am asking each guest to bring a dish to complete the meal. What would you like to bring.*
  - o   Are there any food allergies I need to be aware of?
  - o   Are there any other dietary restrictions I need to be aware of?

- If no...Sorry you will not be able to join us. Hopefully, you will be able to join another group on different date.
  - o   Make note of response - do they want to be invited again?
  - o   Report this information to the Shabbat Dinner Chair.

- Report your guest list to the Shabbat Dinner Chair.

Rabbi's Suggested Service for Home *Shabbat* Dinners

Creating a Place of Welcome

Guide: For this text study, have one participant read aloud the text below. Then use the discussion questions to explore the meaning and how this text is relevant to your own experience.

שוב מעשה בנכרי אחד שבא לפני שמאי, אמר לו: גיירני על מנת שתלמדני כל
התורה כולה כשאני עומד על רגל אחת. דחפו באמת הבנין שבידו. בא לפני הלל,
גייריה. אמר לו: דעלך סני לחברך לא תעביד - זו היא כל התורה כולה, ואידך -
פירושה הוא, זיל גמור.

תלמוד בבלי שבת דף לא.א -

...it happened that a certain non-Jew came before Shammai and said to him, "Take me as a convert, but on condition that you teach me the entire Torah while I stand on one foot." Shammai instantly drove him away with a builder's measuring rod he happened to have in his hand. When the non-Jew came before Hillel, Hillel said to him, "What is hateful to you, do not do to your fellow human. This is the entire Torah, all of it; the rest is commentary. Go and study it."

- Babylonian Talmud, Shabbat 31a

Background
Shabbat is a tractate of the Babylonian Talmud, the quintessential collection of the rabbinic oral tradition, edited in Babylonia around the year 500 CE. Hillel and Shammai were the two great rabbis and teachers of their generation, in the first century BCE. Each one had a group of disciples, who followed the tenets of their lead rabbi. Hillel and Shammai are often depicted as representing opposite views within the Jewish world.

Questions for Discussion

1) Why was Shammai upset by the non-Jew's request?

2) We often hear Hillel's statement in the reverse: Do unto others as you would want done unto you. In what ways are the two statements different? The same?

3) How is it possible that this one statement represents the meaning of the entire Torah?

4) What can we learn from Hillel's approach to the potential convert, as opposed to Shammai? How is this lesson useful in building One Family?

HOST:

We begin by connecting with our companions. Before Shabbat begins, take a moment to reflect on where you have been over the course of the last week. Think through the days, one by one, and remember what you have accomplished. Accept the challenges that you have faced, and learn from those experiences. Celebrate your successes, and strive to replicate those outcomes. Focus on a particularly meaningful experience from your week. In a moment we will go around and share something from the days that past. It may be a triumph, a hurdle that caused us to stumble, or other news from our lives.

[HOST SHARES AND THEN GOES AROUND TABLE TO INVITE OTHERS TO SHARE.]

READER:

Each of these experiences shaped our lives, and added to our journeys. Thank you God for helping us to reach these sacred moments in our lives, and for the opportunity to share them with our friends.

ALL:

בָּרוּךְ אַתָּה, יי אֱלֹהֵינוּ, מֶלֶךְ הָעוֹלָם, שֶׁהֶחֱיָנוּ וְקִיְּמָנוּ וְהִגִּיעָנוּ לַזְּמַן הַזֶּה.

BA-RUCH A-TAH ADONAI, ELOHEINU ME-LECH HA-OLAM, SHE-HECH-AY-YANU, V'KI-A-MANU, V'HIG-EE-ANU, LAZ-MAN HA-ZEH.

We praise You, *Adonai* our God, Ruler of the universe, who has given us life, sustained us, and brought us to this joyous time. Amen.

The Israeli writer Ahad Ha'am taught, "More than Israel has kept Shabbat, Shabbat has kept Israel." Marking this sacred time in our week unites us as a people, and links us with generations past. As we kindle these Shabbat candles, so may their light illumine our lives, and kindle within us the spark needed to engage in a life of blessing.

[CANDLES ARE LIT.]

READER:

בָּרוּךְ אַתָּה יְיָ אֱלֹהֵינוּ מֶלֶךְ הָעוֹלָם, אֲשֶׁר קִדְּשָׁנוּ בְּמִצְוֹתָיו, וְצִוָּנוּ לְהַדְלִיק נֵר שֶׁל שַׁבָּת.

Ba-rukh a-tah Adonai, E-lo-hey-nu me-lekh ha-o-lahm, a-sheyr kid-sha-nu b'mitz-vo-tav v'tzee-va-nu l'had-leek neyr shel Sha-bat.

We praise You, Eternal God, Sovereign of the universe: You hallow us with Your mitzvot, and command us to kindle the lights of Shabbat.

READER:

The candles signify the start of a new time. Now we raise our glasses as we sanctify this time of Shabbat with a blessing over the fruit of the vine.

בָּרוּךְ אַתָּה יְיָ אֱלֹהֵינוּ מֶלֶךְ הָעוֹלָם, בּוֹרֵא פְּרִי הַגָּפֶן.

Ba-rukh a-ta, Adonai, e-lo-hey-nu me-lekh ha-o-lahm, bo-rey p'ree ha-ga-fen.

בָּרוּךְ אַתָּה יְיָ אֱלֹהֵינוּ מֶלֶךְ הָעוֹלָם, אֲשֶׁר קִדְּשָׁנוּ בְּמִצְוֹתָיו וְרָצָה בָנוּ, וְשַׁבָּת קָדְשׁוֹ בְּאַהֲבָה וּבְרָצוֹן הִנְחִילָנוּ זִכָּרוֹן לְמַעֲשֵׂה בְרֵאשִׁית, כִּי הוּא יוֹם תְּחִלָּה לְמִקְרָאֵי קֹדֶשׁ, זֵכֶר לִיצִיאַת מִצְרָיִם.

Ba-rukh a-ta, Adonai, e-lo-hey-nu me-lekh ha-o-lahm, a-sher kid-sha-nu b'mitz-vo-tav v'ra-tzah va-nu, v'Sha-bat kod-sho b'a-ha-vah oov-ra-tzon hin-khee-la-nu, zee-ka-ron l'ma-a-seh v'rey-sheet. Kee hu yom t'khee-lah l'meek-ra-ey ko-desh, ze-kheyr lee-tzee-at mitz-ra-yim.

כִּי בָנוּ בָחַרְתָּ וְאוֹתָנוּ קִדַּשְׁתָּ מִכָּל הָעַמִּים, וְשַׁבַּת קָדְשְׁךָ בְּאַהֲבָה וּבְרָצוֹן הִנְחַלְתָּנוּ.

Kee va-nu va-khar-ta v'o-tah-nu kee-dash-ta mee-kol ha-a-mim, v'Sha-bat kod-sh'kha b'a-ha-vah oov-rah-tzon hin-khal-ta-nu.

בָּרוּךְ אַתָּה יְיָ, מְקַדֵּשׁ הַשַּׁבָּת.

Ba-rukh a-ta, Adonai, m'ka-deysh ha-Sha-bat.

We praise You, God, Ruler of the universe, Creator of the fruit of the vine. We praise You, Adonai, Ruler of the universe, for delighting in us and sanctifying us with Your mitzvot. Lovingly, You have given us Your holy Shabbat as an inheritance and a reminder of Creation and the Exodus from Egypt. It is first among our sacred days. You have chosen us from all people and have given us a sacred purpose in life. Lovingly, you have given us Your holy Shabbat as a sacred heritage. Praised are You, O God, who makes Shabbat holy.

[THE CHALLAH IS UNCOVERED]

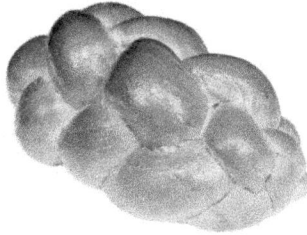

READER:
Before we eat our meal, we offer thanksgiving to God.

*Ba-rukh a-ta, Adonai E-lo-hey-nu, me-lekh
ha-o-lahm, ha-mo-tzee le-khem min
ha-a-retz.*

בָּרוּךְ אַתָּה יְיָ אֱלֹהֵינוּ מֶלֶךְ
הָעוֹלָם, הַמּוֹצִיא לֶחֶם מִן הָאָרֶץ.

Blessed are you, Adonai our God, Ruler of the Universe, who brings forth bread from the earth.

READER:
Shabbat is a time for friends and family to be together. We are grateful to the
hosts for their hospitality, which is in the spirit of our ancestors, Abraham
and Sarah. May this home always be a place of blessing and peace.

ADDITIONAL SONGS:

V'SHAMRU · ושמרו

וְשָׁמְרוּ בְנֵי יִשְׂרָאֵל אֶת הַשַּׁבָּת, לַעֲשׂוֹת אֶת הַשַּׁבָּת לְדֹרֹתָם בְּרִית
עוֹלָם. בֵּינִי וּבֵין בְּנֵי יִשְׂרָאֵל אוֹת הִיא לְעֹלָם, כִּי שֵׁשֶׁת יָמִים עָשָׂה
יְיָ אֶת הַשָּׁמַיִם וְאֶת הָאָרֶץ, וּבַיּוֹם הַשְּׁבִיעִי שָׁבַת וַיִּנָּפַשׁ.

*V'sham-ru v'ney Yisrael et ha-sha-bat, la-a-sot et ha-sha-bat l'do-ro-tahm b'rit o-lahm.
Bey-nee u-veyn b'ney Yisrael ot hee l'o-lahm. kee shey-shet ya-meem a-sah Adonai et
ha-sha-ma-yim v'et ha-a-retz, u-va-yom hash-vee-ee sha-vat va-yee-na-fahsh.*

The people of Israel shall keep the Sabbath, observing the Sabbath in every generation, as a covenant for all time. It
is a sign forever between Me and the people of Israel, for in six days God made heaven and earth, and on the
seventh day God rested and was refreshed.

THE JOY OF SHABBAT - YISMACHU · ישמחו

יִשְׂמְחוּ בְמַלְכוּתְךָ שׁוֹמְרֵי שַׁבָּת וְקוֹרְאֵי עֹנֶג. עַם מְקַדְּשֵׁי שְׁבִיעִי, כֻּלָּם
יִשְׂבְּעוּ וְיִתְעַנְּגוּ מִטּוּבֶךָ, וְהַשְּׁבִיעִי רָצִיתָ בּוֹ וְקִדַּשְׁתּוֹ, חֶמְדַּת יָמִים אוֹתוֹ
קָרָאתָ, זֵכֶר לְמַעֲשֵׂה בְרֵאשִׁית.

*YIS-MA-CHU V'MAL'CHUT-CHA SHOM-REI SHA-BAT V'KO-REI O-NEG. AM M'KA-D'SHEI SH'VI-I,
KU-LAM YIS-BA-U V'YIT-AN-GU MI-TU-VECH-A, V'HASH-VI-I RA-TZI-TA BO V'KI-DASH-TO,
CHEM-DAT YA-MIM O-TO KA-RA-TA, ZE-CHER L'MA-A-SEH V'REI-SHIT.*

Those who keep the Sabbath and call it a delight shall rejoice in Your deliverence. All who
hallow the seventh day shall be gladdened by Your goodness. This day is Israel's festival of the
spirit, sanctified and blessed by You; the most precious of days, a symbol of the joy of Creation.

APPENDIX 3A-5
The Voice[b] Article – Shabbat Home Dinners
February 2016

HOME SHABBAT DINNERS with STRINGS ATTACHED!

Temple Shalom's Home Shabbat Dinner Committee, a One Family activity, announces a new twist to home-held Shabbat Dinners – **Shabbat Dinner Trains!** This is how it works: Each host couple, family, or single will invite one, two, or more other couple(s), family(ies), or single(s) to their home for Shabbat Dinner…with a string attached. The invitees can be friends of the hosts or someone they do not know or know well (a friendly environment for developing new relationships!) The <u>string</u> is that the invited guests are asked to host a Shabbat Dinner in their home, with their guests also being asked to host a Shabbat Dinner in their home, and so on, creating a <u>string</u> of Shabbat Dinners – a **Shabbat Dinner Train!** The trains will be colorfully displayed in the Temple. Each host family name (with permission) will appear on a train car, the cars being connected by… **strings!**

Some guidelines:

- Hosts select a date that is convenient for them,
- Hosts select the number of guests to invite, deciding whether to invite one, two, or more other single(s), couple(s), or family(ies).
- Hosts choose the style of their dinner – COOK OUT, CARRY OUT, POT LUCK, CHINESE, ITALIAN, ISRAELI, or TRADITIONAL, etc.
- Remember, this is an opportunity to share Shabbat with other Temple families in a relaxed home environment. Including someone you don't know well reflects the "audacious hospitality" that is Temple Shalom! Hosts can contact the Shabbat Dinner Chair for names of members who want to participate in this program.
- Hosts need to notify the leader of the Home Shabbat Dinner Committee for their dinner to be a part of an official Shabbat Dinner Train.
- Those who have already hosted Shabbat Dinners will be included in the train displays. Of course, if hosts choose to invite a larger group without strings, as was done in the past, they will also be included in the displays.

Start a Shabbat Dinner Train and watch it grow!

Article in *The Shabbat Shalom*[a] – *Shabbat* Home Dinners

July 20, 2016

Home Shabbat Dinner Program

Would you like to share a Shabbat dinner with others in a relaxed home setting?

Would you like to be a host to others for a Shabbat dinner?

Dinners can be potluck, home cooked or order in. It's all about being together and getting to know other Temple Shalom members.

If you would like to be a Shabbat dinner host or attend a Shabbat dinner, please call.

Article in *The Voice*[b] – Home *Shabbat* Dinners Return

June/July 2018

HOME SHABBAT DINNERS

We are happy to announce that the Shabbat Dinner Train is back!

Shabbat home dinners provide an opportunity to share Shabbat with other Temple members and families in a relaxed home environment. It's a wonderful experience that enhances the One Family philosophy.

How it works:
- A host family invites two or more couples/singles to their home for Shabbat dinner
- Invitees should include established and new members
- After shared dinner where new bonds may be formed the guests are then asked to host a Shabbat dinner in their home
- Hosts can choose any style of dinner - pot luck, traditional, carry out, Chinese, etc.

Past Shabbat Dinner Train participants are displayed on the wall near the library in the Temple. Stop by and take a look.

Let's get the trains chugging again!

If you would like to be a Shabbat Dinner Train host, or if you would like more information, please contact

---

APPENDIX 3A-8

Shabbat Tables Brochure

W<small>ELCOMING</small> S<small>HABBAT TO YOUR HOME</small>

SHABBAT TABLES
You're Invited!

More than Jews have kept Shabbat,
Shabbat has kept the Jews.
Ahad Ha'am

Temple Shalom
One family, many connections

It is customary to light candles before the time of sunset, the official start of Shabbat. For many years, the lighting of Shabbat candles was a woman's domain. Today, this ritual can include whoever chooses to light candles. Two candles are lit, one for each mention of Shabbat in the listing of the Ten Commandments in the Torah, *Exodus 20.8, Deuteronomy 5.12*. Many families add a candle for each child and light them all together as a family.

"As these candles give light to all who behold them, so may we by our lives, give light to all who behold us. As their brightness reminds us of the generations of Israel who have kindled light, so may we, in our own way, be among those who kindle light."

Light candles and then say the following blessing:

| Blessed are You, Eternal our God, Sovereign of the Universe. You hallow us with Your mitzvot and command us to kindle the lights of Shabbat. | בָּרוּךְ אַתָּה יְיָ, אֱלֹהֵינוּ מֶלֶךְ הָעוֹלָם, אֲשֶׁר קִדְּשָׁנוּ בְּמִצְוֹתָיו וְצִוָּנוּ לְהַדְלִיק נֵר שֶׁל שַׁבָּת. | Baruch Atah Adonai, Eloheinu Melech haolam, asher kid'shanu b'mitzvotav v'tzivanu l'hadlik ner shel Shabbat. |

May we be blessed with Sabbath joy.
May we be blessed with Sabbath peace.
May we be blessed with Sabbath light.

You may want to read this following the candle blessing:

We give thanks for family and home. May it be warm with love and companionship. Here may we always find rest from the day's work, and refuge from cares; may our joys be deepened and our griefs softened by the love we give and receive.

Why do people sometimes cover their eyes when they say the blessing over the candles? In most cases, the Hebrew blessing is said before we fulfill a ritual act. When we recite the blessing over candles, we are declaring Shabbat to have begun. Once Shabbat has officially started, traditional practice forbids lighting a fire. Because of this, many people cover their eyes so they cannot see the burning candles until after the blessing has been recited.

K iddush means "sanctification." It comes from the same Hebrew root as the word *kadosh*, which means "holy." "Remember the Sabbath day to keep it holy" (to sanctify it). *Exodus 20.8* Judaism uses wine or grape juice, a symbol of joy and life, to sanctify time. Some stand during *Kiddush*, others sit.

"Six days shall you labor and do all your work, but the seventh day is consecrated to Adonai your God." With wine, our symbol of joy, we celebrate this day and its holiness. We give thanks for all our blessings, for life and health, for work and rest, for home and love and friendship. On Shabbat, eternal sign of creation, we rejoice that we are created in the divine image.

Raise the cup(s) of wine, say the blessing and drink the wine.
Although it is suggested to sing/say the entire kiddush, some people recite only the first sentence.

We bless You, Eternal God, Sovereign of the universe, Creator of the fruit of the vine.	בָּרוּךְ אַתָּה יְיָ, אֱלֹהֵינוּ מֶלֶךְ הָעוֹלָם, בּוֹרֵא פְּרִי הַגָּפֶן.	Baruch Atah Adonai, Eloheinu melech haolam, borei p'ri hagafen.

Interpretive Translation:
Blessed are You, Eternal God, Sovereign of the universe: You call us to sanctity with the Mitzvah of Shabbat – the sign of Your love, a reminder of Your creative work, and the freedom from Egyptian bondage: our day of days. On Shabbat especially, we respond to Your call to serve You as a holy people. We praise You, Adonai, for the holiness of Shabbat.

בָּרוּךְ אַתָּה יְיָ, אֱלֹהֵינוּ מֶלֶךְ הָעוֹלָם, אֲשֶׁר קִדְּשָׁנוּ בְּמִצְוֹתָיו וְרָצָה בָנוּ, וְשַׁבַּת קָדְשׁוֹ בְּאַהֲבָה וּבְרָצוֹן הִנְחִילָנוּ, זִכָּרוֹן לְמַעֲשֵׂה בְרֵאשִׁית. כִּי הוּא יוֹם תְּחִלָּה לְמִקְרָאֵי־קֹדֶשׁ, זֵכֶר לִיצִיאַת מִצְרָיִם. כִּי בָנוּ בָחַרְתָּ וְאוֹתָנוּ קִדַּשְׁתָּ מִכָּל־הָעַמִּים, וְשַׁבַּת קָדְשְׁךָ בְּאַהֲבָה וּבְרָצוֹן הִנְחַלְתָּנוּ. בָּרוּךְ אַתָּה יְיָ, מְקַדֵּשׁ הַשַּׁבָּת.

Baruch Atah Adonai, Eloheinu melech ha-olam, asher kid'shanu b'mitzvotav v'ratza vanu, v'shabat kod'sho b'ahava uv'ratzon hinchilanu, zikaron l'ma'asei v'reisheet. Ki hu yom t'chila l'mikra'ei kodesh, zecher litziat Mitzrayim. Ki vanu vacharta v'otanu kidashta mikol ha'amim, v'shabat kod'sh'cha b'ahava uv'ratzon hin'chaltanu. Baruch Atah Adonai, m'kadeish hashabat.

Does the Kiddush prayer, or any of the prayers, need to be said in Hebrew?
Although Hebrew is preferred, it is acceptable to say the Kiddush prayer, and any prayer, in English or any other language. Kiddush means sanctification, and when we sanctify the wine at the start of the Sabbath meal, in whatever language, we separate and elevate this moment from all the other times during the week when we might drink wine. And like the lighting of the candles, all are welcome to join in the Kiddush prayer.

Blessing over the bread - Ha'Motzi

Challah is the special bread for Shabbat. Even in the poor homes of Eastern Europe where the daily fare was rough black bread, on Shabbat the bread was a special loaf of white flour and eggs. Some people wash their hands before eating the *challah*, not for cleanliness, but to remind us that eating has spiritual potential. Washing forces us to slow down and be grateful for the food we are about to eat.

Say the blessing and eat the bread.

Blessed are You, Eternal our God, Sovereign of the universe: who brings forth bread from the earth.

בָּרוּךְ אַתָּה יְיָ,
אֱלֹהֵינוּ מֶלֶךְ הָעוֹלָם,
הַמּוֹצִיא לֶחֶם
מִן־הָאָרֶץ.

Baruch Atah Adonai,
Eloheinu melech haolam,
hamotzi lechem
min ha'aretz.

Why do some people cover the challah bread(s) with a cloth? As one looks at the Shabbat table, one notices that the Shabbat candles are in beautiful candlesticks and that the wine is held up in a lovely Kiddush cup. While the blessings over them are being recited, the challah lies alone on the table. The Rabbis, seeing this, decreed that the challah should be covered, lest its feelings be hurt by its seemingly secondary status. One rabbi said: "This teaches us concern for the feelings even of inanimate things. And if this is the case, how much more so we should be concerned about the feelings of human beings." Thus, we cover the challot as a lesson in human dignity.

There is a tradition that no knife should be used to cut the challah as a reminder of the prophetic verse: "And they shall beat their swords into plowshares and their spears into pruning hooks" *Isaiah 2:4*.

Blessing after the Meal – Birkat Ha'Mazon

Some families may wish to say a blessing of thanks at the end of the Sabbath meal – just as they began the meal with thanks. It's easy to stop before a meal and say thank you. The sign of true gratitude is to stop when you are full and count your blessings. That is the idea behind *Birkat Hamazon*. "When you have eaten and are satisfied, then you shall bless Adonai, your God, for the good land God has given you." *Deuteronomy 8.10*

Blessed are You, Adonai, who feeds all.

*Baruch Atah Adonai
Ha-Zan et ha-kol*

SHABBAT TABLES
You're Invited!

Whether celebrating Shabbat is something you grew up with, or something new for you and your family, we hope the information you find here will be helpful as you welcome members of Temple Sinai to your home for a Shabbat meal together as part of Shabbat Tables. We'd like to hear from you if you have any ideas or comments. Please email Ana Maria Tamargo, Membership Engagement Coordinator at atamargo@naplestemple.org. Thank you for being a part of Shabbat Tables.

When most people think of holidays, they think of annual celebrations, but in Judaism there is one holiday that occurs every week – the Sabbath. Shabbat, the only holiday mentioned in the Ten Commandments, truly has been a unifying force for Jews the world over. It is a chance to pause, reflect, and differentiate between the holy and the mundane. We hope that Shabbat Tables will help you set this time apart - to make it in some way different and special.

We are commanded to remember and observe Shabbat; this means more than merely not forgetting to observe Shabbat. It also means to remember the significance of Shabbat – we rejoice in the creation of the physical universe, and God's rest on the seventh day – and we are reminded of our own experience of slavery and the freedom we enjoy.

The model of Sabbath rest can be found in Genesis: "The heaven and earth were finished, and all their array. On the seventh day God finished the work which God had been doing, and God rested on the seventh day from all the work which God had done. And God blessed the seventh day and declared it holy, because on it God rested from all the work of creation which God had done." *Genesis 2.1-3*

Thus, the pattern of work and rest is woven into the very fabric of the universe. Rest means more than physical cessation of work. It implies taking oneself out of the ordinary, out of the rat race. This kind of rest gives us the opportunity to re-create our spirit and restore our soul. Shabbat is a time that is set aside to take notice of the wonders around us.

We ask, that as part of Shabbat Tables, each household say 3 blessings:
- The blessing over the candles, to welcome Shabbat
- The blessing over the wine, to sanctify Shabbat
- The blessing over the bread, to begin the Shabbat meal

God rested on the seventh day and took the time to admire all that was created. Shabbat encourages us to take time and look back at the week past and enjoy family and friends around our Shabbat table.

The principle of Shabbat is to sanctify time. The whole of Shabbat is greater than the sum of its parts. It is more than lighting candles, drinking wine, attending a service or eating challah. We sanctify Shabbat by setting it apart, making it distinct from the rest of our week. As Abraham Joshua Heschel has written: "Six days a week we live under the tyranny of things of space; on the Sabbath we try to become attuned to holiness in time."

We offer thanks, O God, for this Shabbat which unites us in faith and hope.
　　　　For Shabbat holiness, which inspires sacred living,
　　　　For Shabbat memories, glowing even in darkness,
　　　　For Shabbat peace, born of friendship and love, We
　　　　offer thanks and blessing, O God.
　　　　Mishkah T'filah, Shabbat Morning Service

Shabbat Tables is an exciting initiative at Temple Shalom where members invite other members to their homes for a Shabbat meal together. It's one way we at Temple Shalom more fully realize our mission of fostering connections one to another, Temple, Israel, Torah and God.

If you are interested in learning more about Shabbat Tables, please call.

Temple
Shalom
One family, many connections

APPENDIX 3B

Article in *The Voice*[b] – Tribute Garden

June/July 2017

Temple Shalom
One family, many connections

Dedication opportunities for the Tribute Garden

Preparing the Ground

The summer of 2015 witnessed the completion of the Temple Shalom Tribute Garden Phase I. With the help of generous donations, we removed the three oaks trees—which were becoming a nuisance and an eyesore—and beautified the space with a new patio garden. As you may remember, we started the project with the final goal of transforming the area into a Tribute Garden for the whole community to enjoy. The Temple Shalom board of trustees is pleased to announce the plans for the final phase.

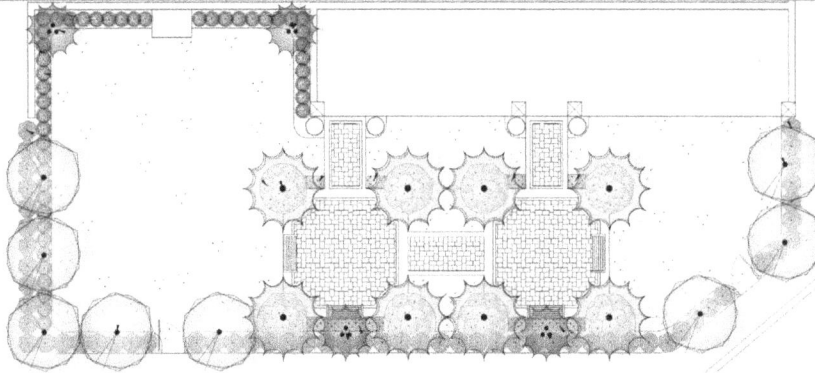

Designing a Space for Community

Our new Building & Grounds Committee began planning the Tribute Garden's final phase earlier this year. We decided to create a space where one can pay tribute to the past through reflection and meditation, as well as celebrate the future with a space that can accommodate multiple uses.

As you can see from the new plans, Phase II is designed with the features needed to create a practical and peaceful place for our community. We will expand the paver patio to provide space for larger events, and use new landscaping features to shield the garden from the parking lot. The plan also leaves the area north of the garden open for future plantings, and for landscape lighting.

Dedicating the Tribute Garden Together

We want to make the Temple Shalom Tribute Garden a space everyone can share. In the final design, the Building & Grounds Committee included three separate opportunities for members to help support the garden through a formal dedication: garden benches— four are initially proposed, existing and newly planted trees, and an area of the patio for engraved pavers.

- $ _____ donation to dedicate a bench in the Temple Shalom Tribute Garden

- $ _____ donation to dedicate an existing or newly planted tree in the Temple Shalom Tribute Garden

- $ _____ donation for one 12"X12" personalized paver - 8 lines, up to 20 characters per line

- $ _____ donation for an 8"x8" personalized engraved paver - 6 lines, up to 20 characters per line

- $ _____ donation for an 4"x8" personalized engraved paver - 3 lines, up to 20 characters per line

Pavers to be placed in a special area of the Tribute Garden

Each phase of our Tribute Garden would be impossible without your generous support.
We hope you will take this opportunity to help make Temple Shalom beautiful and inviting for all of our members.

Help support the Tribute Garden by filling out this form and returning it with your payment to the Temple office

Please make your selection below.

____ $ _____ donation to dedicate a bench in the Tribute Garden. *

____ $ _____ donation to dedicate an existing or newly planted tree in the Tribute Garden. *

____ $ _____ donation for one 12"x12" personalized paver. *

____ $ _____ donation for one 8" x 8" personalized paver 6 lines, up to 20 characters/spaces per line

____ $ _____ donation for one 4"x 8" personalized paver 3 lines, up to 20 characters/spaces per line

* We will contact you for dedication wording.

Please provide your wording for your paver in the spaces below. **Please print clearly.** *If you've ordered more than one paver, use a separate sheet of paper and attach it to this form.*

Name_____
Address_____
_____
Phone_____

My check for $_____ is enclosed
Please bill my credit card for $ _____
Card #_____ Exp_____
Name & billing address *if different than above*   CVC_____
_____
_____
_____
_____

1																			
2																			
3																			
4																			
5																			
6																			

TEMPLE SHALOM
Naples

APPENDIX 3C

Article in *The Voice*[b] – iTemple Launch

February 2016

iTemple is being launched to the entire Temple Shalom community by February 5th.

iTemple is a *private, members-only* Temple Shalom platform.

Your invitation will come by email. Sign up and take the fun surveys to learn who else in our Temple Shalom community has interests similar to yours. If you like to play golf, you can start a group called golfing and invite others to join you for a round or two. Maybe you'd like to start a *havurah* and want to find members in your age group. You can do that! Thinking of having a BBQ? You can send invitations right from iTemple and get RSVPs that way also. One of our members has already started a popular group for dance lessons!

iTemple is a great way to connect with other members as well as get messages targeted to your interests. It's fun and really easy to use, but, we know that some members might need a hand to learn their way around iTemple to feel completely comfortable using it. We've got you covered. There will be informational workshops for hands on experience. Stay tuned for information on dates and times.

In the meantime, try it out! Don't worry, you won't break it! :-)

APPENDIX 3D-1

Article in *The Voice*[b] – Hearing Loop/ First Request for Financial Support

December 2015

TEMPLE SHALOM ANNOUNCES THE HEARING LOOP PROJECT

In the spirit of One Family at Temple Shalom, we are prepared to implement the installation of a "loop" system in our sanctuary. We have ensured that the sanctuary meets the standards required for the system and the Board of Trustees has approved this installation. We believe this system will enhance the experience of worship and event participation for many of our members who use hearing aids. The loop system consists of hidden wires around the sanctuary that connect to our current sound system. Those who have hearing aids with a telecoil ("t" switch) will receive amplified sound directly into their hearing aids. For those whose hearing aids do not have a telecoil, compatible headsets will be provided.

Many places of worship in Naples have installed a loop system and their members have praised the clarity of sound it provides. Providing this enhancement for Temple Shalom members who have a hearing loss will help to ensure that their Temple experience is the best that it can be.

But, we need your help! The system will cost $6,000 including installation. We are looking for donations to fund this project. If you have a hearing loss, if you wear a hearing aid, if you have family members with a hearing loss, perhaps you would like to support installation of the loop system. Of course, anyone who is concerned about providing handicapped accessibility might also help. We are grateful for donations of any amount.

Article in *The Voice*[b] – Hearing Loop/ Last Request for Financial Support

January 2017

Hear Ye!   Hear Ye!

The Hearing Loop is Now Available for Use in our Sanctuary!

This Loop is designed to be used with hearing aids that are equipped with a telecoil (T-switch). A wire loop, installed under the carpet around the stationary seats in our Sanctuary, is connected directly to the microphones. The wire transmits sound electromagnetically to the telecoil in personal hearing aids. This system provides quality sound using the personalized settings of individual hearing aids.

For those who do not have hearing aids or whose hearing aids do not have a telecoil, headsets compatible with the Loop system are available on the table just inside of the sanctuary doors.

There will be an orientation program on Sunday morning, January 22, at 11:45. A local ASHA Board Certified Audiologist, will be available to answer questions and assist with determining if your personal hearing aids are compatible with the Loop.

This important addition to our Temple technology has been made possible by the generosity of our Temple Board of Trustees, Sisterhood, Men's Club, and generous individual members.

Much thanks to all!

Additional donations to complete covering the costs of this system will be appreciated and can be made by sending checks payable to Temple Shalom with a notation for the Loop.

APPENDIX 3D-3

Footnote in *The Shabbat Shalom*[a] – Loop Presence in Sanctuary

September 2016 – Present

Our Sanctuary is equipped with a hearing loop designed for those who have hearing aids with a telecoil (T switch). Large print prayer books and listening devices can be found on the table in the back of the Sanctuary. If you need assistance, please see one of our Shabbat greeters.

Article in *The Voice*[b] – One Family...Many Stories

June/July 2015

One Family...Many Stories

We want to hear your story – your history, your Jewish journey, and...
> What are you passionate about?
> > What are you most proud of?
> > > What attracted you to Temple Shalom?
> > > > What do you love most about Temple Shalom?
> > > > > What can we do better?

You may get a phone call from a member of Temple Shalom asking for 30 minutes of your time. He or she will ask for a face-to-face meeting at your home, a coffee shop or any place that is most convenient for you. We hope you will say YES.

We want to complete 100 of these one-to-one conversations over the remainder of the year with a sampling of our membership. These conversations will help to strengthen existing relationships as well as create new relationships within our Temple community. They will also help us to meet the needs of our congregation as we understand your needs and passions.

We promise to respect your time...we will limit the conversation to 30 minutes...and we will respect your privacy. We know you have an interesting and amazing story and we want to hear it directly from you. If you don't want to wait for a phone call, you can email, or call, one of the following people and we would be thrilled to set up a time and place to meet.

We're excited about getting these one-to-one conversations started...and excited about hearing your story.

Training Meeting Agenda – One Family...Many Stories

Summer – Fall 2015

Agenda
Training for One-to-One Conversations
Thursday, August 13, 2015
1:00 - 2:00 PM

- Introductions

- What we are doing and why

- Key elements of one-to-one conversations

- Conversation guide

- Sample one-to-one conversation

- Sample email and article from The Voice

- Sample form to be completed after each conversation

- Questions

- Next steps
    1. complete 2-3 conversations prior to High Holy Days
    2. List of members to call
    3. Follow up meeting (after HHD)

APPENDIX 3E-3

Background Materials –
One Family...Many Stories

One Family...Many Stories
One-to-One-Training

Why Do One-to-One Conversations

- Strengthen existing relationships and create new relationships within the Temple Shalom family.

- Hearing the passions and stories of our members enable us to connect with others who share the same passions and stories.

- We see people during services or holidays, but we don't know them. A 30-minute conversation changes your relationship.

- Enable Temple Shalom to do a better job in planning events, programs and activities based on shared interest.

What are the Key Elements of a One-to-One Conversation?

- Face to face...not over the phone.

- They are scheduled meetings arranged by phone or in person.

- Conversations should be thirty minutes. Only extend the time if the person you are talking to agrees.

- Usually, it only involves you and one other person. It is OK to include the spouse or partner if they request them to be included.

- The meeting can take place at a coffee shop, the individual's home or wherever it is convenient for you both.

- You should not take notes during the one-to-one. Instead, jot down your observations after you are done and back in your car. A form will be provided.

- It is not a formal interview. It is a conversation.

- Your job is to elicit key stories of the other person's life. Ask open-ended questions.

- LISTEN.

- The person you are talking to should be doing most of the talking. Maybe 70-80% for them and 20-30% for you.

- After you have the conversation, send a thank-you note to the person with whom you met.

Conversation Guide – One Family...Many Stories

Conversation Guide

We want to know more about you:

- ◆ Personal profile:

  - Tell me about yourself -- your children, your parents, your siblings;

  - Where are you from? How long have you lived in the Naples area?

  - Where do you work? What are your hobbies? Your interests? Your passions?

  - Does your family have any special needs with which Temple Shalom can assist you?

  - Will you share your "story" (your Jewish journey) with me? If the member is not forthcoming or doesn't seem to understand what you want, you might stimulate their story with some of these questions . . .

    - ◆ Previous experience in a religious community:
      - ✛ Was Judaism (or other religious faith) a part of your home life in your youth.
      - ✛ Did you have a religious education?
      - ✛ Have you been a member of a religious community (as an adult)?
      - ✛ If yes –
      - ✛ Was it a Jewish congregation? Reform? Another faith? Denomination?
      - ✛ Please share with me some description of your previous experience(s) as a member of a religious community. Did you feel connected to that community? Was there something about that experience you feel strongly about?
      - ✛ How involved were you in the life of the congregation? Was that level of involvement satisfying? Are you looking for more involvement?
      - ✛ If no –
      - ✛ What do you think it means to be a part of a religious community

---

♦ Expectations:

- What were you looking for when you became part of a Temple community?

- Why did you select Temple Shalom?

- Please share what you expect to receive as a part of our Temple community. What do you expect to "get" from the experience?

- How do you see Temple Shalom as a part of your life? How do you see being a part of this community as fitting into your family and your family fitting into this community?

- Do you have any ideas about how Temple Shalom can help you meet these expectations?

Article in *The Voice*[b] – Invitation to Participate in *Shalom Chaverim*

April and September 2017

SHALOM CHAVERIM

"Shalom Chaverim" means hello friends in Hebrew. Shalom Chaverim is also the name of a new and exciting volunteer opportunity at Temple Shalom where Temple volunteers welcome members and guests who come for worship, learning and social opportunities.

Temple Shalom is focused on inclusivity, diversity, openness and welcoming. Shalom Chaverim is a cadre of greeters welcoming and assisting members and guests to our Temple for Erev Shabbat services, helping them with their name tags or badges, providing directions, assisting with seating, prayer books, or hearing assisted devices.

If you are interested in volunteering and becoming a part of Shalom Chaverim, please contact   at
                        . Signing up to be a greeter at the sidewalk, in the lobby or in the sanctuary is easy and only takes a few minutes.

We are a congregation dedicated to "audacious hospitality" and to helping our members connect and engage. Being part of Shalom Chaverim is fun and you will be making a difference to all of those visiting our temple by helping to make their experience at Temple Shalom warm and welcoming.

Shalom Chaverim
An opportunity to be part of
Audacious Hospitality at Temple Shalom

Torah teaches us the importance of "welcoming the stranger:" This concept, repeated many times in our ancient texts, is the basis of *Audacious Hospitality*, an initiative of the Union for Reform Judaism. *Audacious Hospitality* is a spiritual practice focused on inclusivity, diversity, openness, and welcoming. These values, also values of our Temple Shalom One Family, have led to the formation of *Shalom Chaverim* (Temple Shalom Friends), a cadre of greeters welcoming members and guests to Temple Shalom for *Erev Shabbat* services. *Shalom Chaverim* is one more way for Temple Shalom members to put our One Family values into practice.

You will encounter members of *Shalom Chaverim* outside by the curb, in the lobby, in the sanctuary, and at the *Oneg Shabbat*. These warm and smiling greeters are an addition to our usual greeters at the podium in the lobby. *Shalom Chaveri*m members will be available to assist members and guests as they arrive at Temple, to help with name badges, to locate prayer books, to assist those with special needs, and to ensure that guests are welcomed and comfortable.

Shalom Chaverim members sign up online for the dates and assignments of their choice. They can participate as often as is comfortable for them. This volunteer opportunity works equally well

- for long-time members and new members
- for those who are in the Naples area full time and those who are here seasonally
- for those who attend services frequently and for those who attend less often
- for members of all ages

If you would like to join our *Shalom Chaverim* Team, contact the Chairs. They will sign you up and make sure you receive an email with easy instructions and a *Shalom Chaverim* Handbook.

This is a fun and friendly way to do a mitzvah, to live Jewishly, and to be involved in the life of Temple Shalom!

Handbook – *Shalom Chaverim*

Front Cover

Temple Shalom
One family, many connections

SHALOM
CHAVERIM

Handbook

Temple Shalom

Naples

Handbook – *Shalom Chaverim*
Inside Front Cover

Shalom Chaverim is a group of Temple Shalom volunteers who assist the congregation in building sacred community by addressing the need for welcoming members and guests who come to Temple Shalom for worship, learning, and social opportunities. With a warm greeting and friendly attentiveness, Shalom Chaverim is dedicated to the mitzvah of *hachnasat orchim*, the offering of hospitality.

Handbook – *Shalom Chaverim*

Page One

Temple Shalom is a congregation dedicated to "*Audacious Hospitality*" and to helping our members *connect and engage*. Audacious hospitality, an initiative of the Union for Reform Judaism, is a spiritual practice focused on inclusivity, diversity, openness, and welcoming. These values, embraced by our Temple Shalom One Family, have led to the formation of **Shalom Chaverim** (Temple Shalom Friends), a cadre of greeters welcoming and assisting members and guests to Temple Shalom for erev Shabbat services.

For erev Shabbat services (and soon, other special events taking place at temple), up to five **Shalom Chaverim** members (in addition to our regular Shabbat greeters) will welcome and assist attendees. Beginning outside at the curb in front of our building, continuing in the lobby and in the sanctuary, and throughout the Oneg Shabbat, attendees will be received warmly and assisted with name badges and prayer books, introduced to others, and welcomed to our temple home. Assistance will be provided for individuals with special needs (such as large print prayer books or amplification devices).

Each individual who participates as a **Shalom Chaverim** member signs up for dates they are available and selects a specific assignment. A written description of the assignments can be found in this handbook. Each week the Team Leaders will send a reminder to the Shalom Chaverim members assigned to that week.

The goal of the **Shalom Chaverim** system is to ensure that everyone who enters our temple home feels welcomed and valued and in doing so we create an energy and warmth that is felt by everyone, before, during and after the services. Members of **Shalom Chaverim** truly make it possible for all of us at Temple Shalom to fulfill the mitzvah of *hachnasat orchim* – hospitality.

Handbook – *Shalom Chaverim*

Page Two

Roles for Shalom Chaverim Members

We are welcoming our members and guests to our temple home. Our goal is to provide a warm and friendly atmosphere for all who enter, members and guests alike. When it is your Shabbat to be "on duty" as a Shabbat Shalom greeter, it is incumbent upon you to be reaching out to those you do not know. This is not a time to just visit with friends.

Front sidewalk – One Chaverim member
- Greet and welcome (e.g. "Shabbat Shalom!", "Good Shabbas", "Welcome to Temple Shalom," say something personal...)
- Assist people out of cars, as needed. Help with walkers, wheelchairs, etc. as needed
- If it is raining, hold umbrella over people and walk them to front door (umbrellas are near handicapped entrance doors). Assist people bringing umbrellas to place them in an umbrella bag, located outside handicapped entrance doors

In Lobby – One Chaverim member
- Greet and welcome
- Stand near name badge cabinet
- Assist with finding member name badges, as needed
- Provide directions as needed

In Lobby – One Chaverim member
- Greet and welcome
- Stand near center table located near Shabbat greeters
- Assist with guest name badges
- Provide directions as needed

Handbook – *Shalom Chaverim*

Page Three

In Sanctuary – Two Chaverim members

- Greet and welcome
- Assist with seating as needed
- If guests arrive alone, seating them with members and make introductions
- Assist with prayer books (often confused with Torah books)
- Assist with large print prayer books and assisted hearing devices which are located on the table inside the sanctuary entrance
- Continue standing through opening song to assist and seat late arrivals
- Take note of empty seats when the sanctuary is crowded in order to help worshippers find a seat; ask worshippers to move in when seating is sparse

In Oneg Shabbat – All Chaverim members

- Greet and welcome
- Look for people standing or sitting alone, chat with them and introduce them to others
- Look for guests (identifiable by name badges or by noting who comes forward for the motzi with Rabbi and Cantor in the sanctuary near the end of the service). Chat with them and introduce them to others
- Look for people you do not know and introduce yourself, make a new friend!

Handbook – *Shalom Chaverim*

Page Four

What do I do when it is my turn on Shalom Chaverim?

Contact the Shalom Chaverim Chairs to sign up for a Shabbat.

Preparation for this process is done in coordination with our Membership & Engagement Coordinator. Please mark on your calendar when you have signed up. If something comes up and you cannot make it, **try and switch with someone else on the team**.

The Shalom Chaverim Chairs will send you an email reminder regarding your commitment.

Please be **in place,** wearing your name tag, to welcome people by 6:45pm. Remember, you may be the first impression someone will have of Temple Shalom; impressions count. Shabbat attire, a welcoming smile and a warm greeting are essential each time someone enters our building. We are glad to see them and want to convey that positive feeling of open hospitality.

All Shabbat Chaverim members should be able to assist others with all of the following: location of restrooms, drinking fountain, phone in office, first aid kit and AED (defibrillator) in office copier room and armed security. You should also be able to help visitors with Shabbat Shalom programs, prayer books, Torah commentaries, large print prayer books, hearing assisted devices, name tags and name badges, umbrellas and umbrella bags, kippot and tallit. If you don't know, ask.

Last, but not least, be alert and attentive. At all times, but especially when you are serving as a Shalom Chaverim greeter, pay special attention to others and your surroundings, from the time you arrive in your car until you return to leave. See something unusual or out of place? Say something to the

Handbook – *Shalom Chaverim*

Page Five

security officer or other 'in charge' person. See someone needing assistance or appearing out of sorts? Offer to help or to find assistance. Come across something which requires attention you cannot give? Seek out others to assist you. In short, be our eyes and ears when you are "on duty". You have an important part in ensuring our safety.

Explanation of Hearing Loop System

Our hearing loop was installed in the sanctuary in August 2016. It consists of a wire that is connected to the sound system and circles the stationary seats in the sanctuary. Anyone with a hearing aid that has a telecoil (designed for use with telephones) can switch their hearing aids to the T setting and receive (with very good quality sound) what is being said or sung into the microphones. In order to make use of this technology, the user must be seated within the circle of this loop. It does not include the social hall; it only works in the sanctuary.

We also have headsets that work with the loop system for those who do not have hearing aids with telecoils. These headsets can be found in the loop designated basket located on the table inside the sanctuary entrance. Our FM headsets still work throughout the sanctuary space including in the social hall area. These headsets can be found on the same table in the FM designated basket.

Loop system headsets (We have 4)
Use if they do not have a hearing aid
Use if their hearing aids do not have a telecoil (t-switch)

FM system headsets
Use if loop headsets are all in use.

Thank you so much for participating in this important Temple Shalom One Family experience!

Handbook – *Shalom Chaverim*
Page Six

The Mitzvah of Hospitality

The rabbis of the Talmud and the Midrash saw this mitzvah as very important when it comes to Jewish life. They spoke about this story extensively, and from it they derived one of Judaism's most time-honored and practiced virtues; the virtue of *hachnasat orchim* – the virtue of welcoming the stranger, of offering hospitality.

The Torah is constantly concerned about the well-being of the stranger and, therefore, so were the rabbis. That concern is based upon the fact that, of all people, we as Jews should know what it feels like and what it means, to be a stranger. We know what it is like to be on the outside, looking in. We know what it is like to sometimes feel excluded or ignored or even worse, and we do not like it.

If we do not like being the stranger – the "other" – if we do not like being treated that way, then from our unpleasant experiences we should learn to do better and to be better when we find the tables reversed, when we are the hosts and others are the strangers. If we do not like to be made to feel unwelcome, then it is incumbent upon us to go out of our way to welcome others. It should not matter whether or not they are like us or dramatically different from us. For in the end, as different as we may be, they, like us, are still God's children and should be treated accordingly.

As we welcome strangers into our homes, so should we, as Jews, welcome strangers into our synagogues. *hachnasat orchim* may start in our homes but should naturally flow into our synagogues.

(From the Blog of Rabbi Henry J. Karp)

Handbook – *Shalom Chaverim*

Page Seven

Putting Our Values into Action

Dr. Ron Wolfson, author of *Relational Judaism: Using the Power of Relationships to Transform the Jewish Community*, emphasizes these points for greeters in synagogues:

1. Accepting the Other: The unconditional acceptance of whoever walks into the synagogue is the hallmark of a culture of community. Everyone is made in the image of God. Everyone deserves to be accepted into the community. By offering a handshake and a smile, the gestures say, "You are welcome here." Even if the congregant or visitor responds coldly, it is the task of the greeter "to receive" the person, whatever her/his state of mind is at the time.

2. Recognizing the Other: It takes very little effort to say a good word to people as they come into our Temple home. In addition to the appropriate greeting of the day ("Shabbat Shalom", " Chag Sameach"), and, when you can, add a word or two of a personal nature—"How are the kids?" "How's your Mom doing?" – to recognize the other.

3. Uplifting the Other: Sometimes people come to the synagogue in search of encouragement, comfort and peace. Perhaps they have had a frustrating week. They may be coming to say Kaddish for a loved one. Show tenderness and kindness to those who come to shul. Introduce a visitor/ stranger to someone you know. Make a human connection.

4. Teaching the Other: By greeting everyone warmly, you will establish a "climate" of welcome in the group that assembles. Your model of greeting may very well be picked up by others in the group. This modeling is demonstrated by our Rabbi as he invites everyone to "turn and greet" one another as our services starts.

Handbook – *Shalom Chaverim*
Page Eight

5. Attending to the Needs of the Other:
The physically lost. Be on the lookout for those newcomers and visitors who don't know where anything is in the building. They may be embarrassed to ask where certain things are - the restrooms, or have questions about whether to wear a kippah/tallit.

The physically challenged. People who are disabled may need special help in getting settled in the sanctuary. They may need assistance in locating headsets for the loop system or large-print prayer books.

(Adapted from the writings of Dr. Ron Wolfson)

Parashat Vayera

Abraham was sitting at the door of his tent in the heat of the day when he noticed three strangers approaching. They were angels, but he did not know that at the time. As soon as he saw them, he jumped up and ran to greet them, offering them the hospitality of his home. Though he had no idea who they were, still he bowed down before them and treated them as nobility, calling them "My lords." He offered them a little food and then provided them with a feast of cakes and beef and curds and milk.

Genesis 18-22

Handbook – *Shalom Chaverim*

Inside Back Cover

ברוכים הבאים

Bruchim haba'im

Welcome!

Blessed are those who come!

Handbook – *Shalom Chaverim*
Back Cover

SHAL★M
CHAVERIM

APPENDIX 5A

Summary of Readings

Summary of Materials Regarding
Voluntary Commitment System

Sources: Dan Judson Case Study – **Synergy** and others.
See readings listed on pp. 58 & 59.

Standard Dues Structure

- Asking for dues relief is onerous, humiliating, so some families just leave
- People, especially young people, see dues as a barrier; **feel there is constant tension over money**
- **Forces leaders/staff to act as bill collectors, not like a sacred community**
- **Represents a transactional relationship, not in line with the values and culture of a congregation**
- It is risky not to change
- Not in line with Jewish values

Voluntary Commitment System

- **Introduced by Rabbi Stephen Wise over 100 years ago**
- **Creates a covenantal, Torah-based relationship**
- Members tell Temple what they will pay and *determine a personalized payment schedule*
- Members are informed annually of a sustaining amount (expenses divided by the number of members)
- It is a personal financial decision not questioned or **negotiated** by Temple administration; the amount is no longer a hurdle to affiliation
- It is a positive decision made by each member unit
- $ commitment can vary from year to year
- Emphasizes Temple as a co-op rather than a business
- There is a risk to changing; should not be taken lightly

- **School fees should be kept separate**
- **Some Temples set a minimum $ amount as a guide**
- *Temple finances should be monitored monthly*
- Some Temples give one year free to new members
- Some Temples also provide free HHD tickets with a voluntary donation – giving from the heart
- Key is to create fiercely loyal, well-served members
- **There is recognition for those giving above the sustaining amount**

Resulting Changes

Anecdotal:

- Money is no longer a hurdle
- Better feeling around money in the Temple; redefines the meaning of money
- Very few unpaid pledges; need not chase down money
- No dues relief system needed
- Little in unpaid pledges to write off
- Better budget projections
- Better cash flow
- Increase in the number who increase their giving over old dues system
- A surprising number giving more than sustaining amount
- Changes in donor recognition (recognizing all who give above sustaining amount)
- Less giving to other fundraising but revenue remained the same
- Changes the relationship between Temple and the members—
  + System says we care about you; we want you to have a true stake in what Temple does
  + **Members feel empowered**
  + Changes culture
  + Members feel better about their community
- Happy members are better ambassadors for the Temple; they share positive messages about the Temple

- Members become owners, not consumers
- Temple operates more like a community and less like a business
- Recruiting and retaining members easier
- Promotes transparency
- Possible long-term increase in burden on administrative staff
- Changes in leadership style
    + Proactive
    + Creative and bold
    + Go from putting out fires to taking bold action; changes conversation
    + Thinking in new paradigms
    + **Improved lay-professional relationship**

Empirical:
- **Increase in annual membership (4% average; <0% - 25% range)**
- **Level of engagement and involvement increased (survey)**
- **Perceived value of membership heightened (survey)**
- **More new members but often paying less**
- **Individual members paying more**
- **No problem with "free riders"**

Making the Change

- Pre-requisites
    + **Clergy stability**
    + **Have a "fallback" plan**
    + **Determine readiness of congregation to make the change (Synergy pp.29-30; see readiness tool pp.32-35)**
    + Pre-testing survey to determine baseline (Shnider)
    + Need a vision and goal, strategy, communication plan, and a plan to evaluate impacts
    + Key is to create a fiercely loyal, well-served membership

- Financial reasons to change
    + Abatement [relief] process humiliating
    + Dues system a barrier
    + Voluntary system easier to retain members
    + Voluntary system has better atmosphere around money
- Value-based reasons to change (Torah, equality, inclusion, respect, trust, honor)
    + Aligns financial culture with Jewish values
    + Members see selves as partners, not consumers
    + Removes paternalistic dues abatement system
    + Honors everyone whatever they pay
    + Expression of values and relationship, not a fee for service
- Engagement reasons to change
    + People are partners, not told what to do
    + Members pledge engagement/volunteer commitment and money

Preparing Temple Members for Change
- Introduce during the annual meeting, HHD, or dedicated letter
- Find marketing people to design letters, pledge cards, communication pieces, FAQs, web pages, membership applications, donation forms

Evaluation
- Review membership, revenue, engagement levels, giving patterns, community sentiment (satisfaction)
- Timing – before change for a baseline; 6 months after change; other

Problems Experienced with Change
- Members reducing pledge mid-year
- Members not returning pledge forms
- Cash flow management

Motivation for Temple Involvement
- Nostalgic Judaism no longer a draw

- People do things for two reasons
  + Because they want to
  + Because they must
- Non-Orthodox Jews are not in "have to" group; we must move them to the "want to" group
- We must provide a perceived value; to inspire "kishke level" convictions
- Exchange Theory (Shnider)

Christian Model (mega-churches and Chabad)

- Successful because of passion and vision
- Concept of "stewardship"
- Both groups take Jewish teaching seriously (sense of obligation; Torah talks about tithing, "honor Adonai with our wealth"
- Temple must find comparable Jewishly meaningful language as that used by evangelicals

Other Alternatives (p36 -37, Synergy)

- **Traditional**
  + **Typical synagogue gets 50% to 80% of revenue from dues; still must raise additional funds**
  + **Chief benefit – defined revenue source**
  + **Major challenges**
    - **Misaligned with synagogue values**
    - **Those who pay less feel like second class citizens**
    - **Relief process humiliating**
    - **Additional fundraising often feels burdensome**
- **Fair Share**
  + **Dues pegged to income of member; dues is a percentage of income, usually 1.5% to 2%**
  + **Attempts to be aligned with the Jewish value of economic justice**
  + **Major challenges**
    - **Members sometimes suspected of being untruthful**
    - **If documentation required, feels intrusive**
    - **Contributes to a culture of suspicion**

- Hybrids
    + Base dues of $125 per year and sliding scale above that based on 1% to 1.6% of gross income
    + Suggested sliding scale between 1.5% and 2.5% of annual income with no board oversight or relief process
    + Traditional dues with patron categories of benefits (invitation to events, recognition, HHD tickets)
- Benefactor
    + No dues and minimal fees
    + Congregation runs through development work focused on high-end givers
    + Chabad
    + Major challenges
        ⅄ Community does not share in the responsibility of funding
        ⅄ Necessity for constant development work

APPENDIX 5B

Timeline

TIMELINE FOR IMPLEMENTATION OF PLEDGE SYSTEM		THINGS TO DO
8/24/16	Organize implementation team	Include RS, PS, young and senior members
9/1/16	Develop process and policies	Identify issues to address
	Discuss goals and objectives	
	Review process & materials from other Temples	
	Decide type of material & content	Type of mailings, letter, web, etc.
	Decide method of communication	
	Develop material	
	Identify segmented groups*	
	Identify person-person & person-group contacts	Who contacts & what to say
10/1/16	Have material & information sessions scheduled	
	Train session leaders and leadership team	What message we want to deliver and how
	Training session for staff and professionals	Both segment sessions and mailings
	Start the communication	
11/1/16	Solicit feedback	
	Continue with information sessions	
12/1/16	Task force evaluate feedback	
12/15/16	Start budget process	
1/2/17	Work on continued communication	

		Transparent flow of information to members	
1/15/17	Begin office & accounting processes		Finalize invoices with information
2/15/17	First mailing of letter for commitment & pledge		
3/1/17	Review budgets & make adjustments		
3/31/17	Follow up on letters		
	Budget review & adjustments		
4/15/17	Follow up on pledge commitments		
4/30/17	Annual Meeting		
6/1/17	Continued communication & feedback		
	Follow up on pledges not received		
	Person to person discussions		
7/1/17	New fiscal year starts		

* Suggested segmented groups: top cumulative-giving members (>5K/yr) & honorary members; religious school & preschool parents, young adults age <36 (both single and married; associate and seasonal members; members >50 (will break down further); members >36 and <50 years old (will break down further); members still owing building fund; members on reduced dues

[We were not able to adhere to the dates on this timeline but (loosely) followed the order of activities.]

APPENDIX 6A

Article in *The Voice*[b] – One Family Projects Update
April 2016

The One Family Initiative began two years ago to implement the concept of Relational Judaism as described by Dr. Ron Wolfson in his book by the same name. The author himself was the speaker at our kick-off event! Our focus, then and now, is to create systems and an environment at Temple Shalom that are conducive to engaging and connecting our members to each other and to Temple. Our One Family Team meets, brainstorms, considers options, and provides leadership and volunteers to bring our selections to fruition. To date, we have initiated:

- Name badges and cabinet now in our lobby.
- Home-based Shabbat dinner structure.
- Additional new member engagement opportunities.
- Additional seasonal affiliate opportunities.
- Many Stories – a structure of one-on-one conversations among members.
- Redesigned and redecorated Perman Library with seating and coffee bar.
- Tribute Garden with seating (seating to be done).
- Techie Tutors – a member helping member technology-learning structure.
- Live and archived streaming video of services and events in our sanctuary.
- iTemple – a members only, member-driven computer platform connecting our members.
- Affinity groups for senior singles and for empty nesters (more to come).
- A "hearing loop" (coming soon) in our sanctuary to assist participation of members with hearing impairment.

In addition, the increased contact among our members has led to:

- The development of our Tikkun Olam Council, a development and coordination body for social action work at Temple Shalom.
- The realization of the need for programming for our interfaith families.

All of these additions to our Temple Shalom experience have been led and carried out by our awesome volunteers, our members and our staff. Funding has been provided by the generosity of our members.
If you would like to learn more about the projects listed above or if you would like to become part of the One Family team, please contact one of us. Your input would be most welcome.

One Family Team

APPENDIX 6B

Posters in Lobby – Fall 2014

SHABBAT DINNERS

Go to Dinner

Host a Dinner

ONE FAMILY

DO A MITZVAH

Helping others on Mitzvah Day

And throughout the year!

ONE FAMILY

INTERGENERATIONAL ACTIVITIES

Help us plan ways

For all generations of our

One Family

To share experiences at Temple Shalom

ONE FAMILY

AFFINITY GROUPS

Finding others who share your interests

Like biking, running, playing chess, Torah study, etc.

ONE FAMILY

(Each poster included pictures of congregants engaging in activities. Pictures were not available at the time of compiling this information.)

Trifold

September 2015

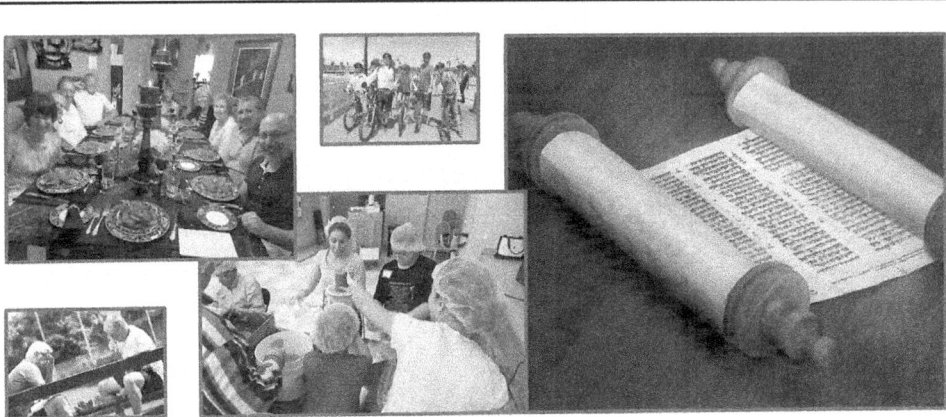

Temple Shalom
4630 Pine Ridge Road
Naples, Florida 34119

✡ ✡ ✡ ✡ ✡ ✡ ✡ ✡ ✡ ✡ ✡ ✡ ✡ ✡ ✡ ✡ ✡ ✡ ✡

One Family
Living a culture of
Connection ▪ Participation ▪ Engagement

✡ ✡ ✡ ✡ ✡ ✡ ✡ ✡ ✡ ✡ ✡ ✡ ✡ ✡ ✡ ✡ ✡ ✡ ✡

For more information or to share your ideas, contact

VOLUNTEER

TEMPLE SHALOM

ONE FAMILY COMES TO LIFE at TEMPLE SHALOM

One Family at Temple Shalom in Naples, Florida, is based on the concepts presented in *Relational Judaism: Using the Power of Relationships to Transform the Jewish Community* (Dr. Ron Wolfson, 2013, Jewish Lights Publishing). In February, 2014, in a gathering of over 300 members, Dr. Wolfson himself introduced the concepts of Relational Judaism to the congregants of Temple Shalom. The response was immediate and enthusiastic. A One Family Team of members was formed. This team acted as a steering committee, brainstorming and prioritizing ideas for a Relational Judaism experience at Temple Shalom. Members of the team also volunteered to lead and work on various projects, bringing the concept of One Family to life. Each of the projects provides a system or a structure that creates opportunities for our members to connect with one another. As the projects were initiated, members of the congregation stepped forward to lead and participate in them. These projects continue to evolve and all members of Temple Shalom are encouraged to participate.

✡ ✡ ✡ ✡ ✡ ✡ ✡ ✡ ✡ ✡ ✡ ✡ ✡ ✡ ✡ ✡ ✡ ✡ ✡ ✡

The One Family Team works in cooperation with many of the existing Temple Shalom committees, projects, and affiliates that were in place and functioning well at the time our process began, including, but not limited to, the following:

Caring Committee	*Building & Grounds*	*Membership*	*Mitzvah Day*
Shabbat Greeters	*Ushers*	*Sisterhood*	*Men's Club*

ONE FAMILY OPPORTUNITIES to ENGAGE IN TEMPLE LIFE

Home-based **Shabbat Dinners** can be scheduled at the convenience of the host. Those who have held or attended one of these dinners have reported having a great experience and developing new relationships with Temple members they might not have otherwise met. Larger group Shabbat Dinners at Temple are also arranged.

Our **Name Badges** are in the beautiful cabinet in our Temple lobby. Be sure to find your badge when you enter the building and to replace it in the cabinet as you are leaving. These name badges are helping us to learn the names of other members, to integrate new members, and to identify our guests.

Ambassadors, an expansion of our Shabbat Greeters and Ushers groups, reaches out to members and guests at events and services to ensure a warm welcome and well-being of all who enter our Temple home.

iTemple, a social networking service, is our Temple Shalom on-line community. Members can create their own profiles, identify their interests, develop new relationships and Affinity Groups, enhancing their ability to connect and engage with one another.

Techie Tutors provides opportunities for non-techie adults to meet with Temple teens who are technologically savvy for the purpose of learning how to make better use of their computers, notepads, or smart phones.

One Family…Many Stories involves one-to-one 30-minute meetings of Conversation Leaders and randomly selected Temple members, providing an opportunity to learn our members' stories – their Jewish journeys, interests, passions, concerns, and expectations. The information gleaned from these conversations will be helpful in planning future programs and developing Affinity Groups.

Streaming Video of services, activities, and events in the sanctuary are available, live, through a link on our website (www.naplestemple.org). In addition, all of the videos are archived, enabling members to view the events from wherever they are and whenever they want.

Our new connection-friendly **Perman Library** is in place and in use. The Library is not only the home of our lending library, but it is the location of the Temple Bean (our coffee station) as well. Stop in, see how beautifully designed and decorated this space is as you meet with other members, browse the book collection, and enjoy a cup of coffee.

The **Tribute Garden,** just outside the social hall, enables our members to meet and chat with others or to meditate outdoors in a soothing and informal atmosphere. Members will be able to honor and remember their loved ones in this garden.

✡ ✡ ✡ ✡ ✡ ✡ ✡ ✡ ✡ ✡ ✡ ✡ ✡ ✡ ✡ ✡ ✡ ✡ ✡ ✡

APPENDIX 6D

Annual Report

2017

ONE FAMILY INITIATIVE
Annual Report – 2017

Relational Judaism, implemented as One Family at Temple Shalom, is a way of thinking, a way of doing things. It is who we strive to be. At Temple Shalom, we are in a transformation, a cultural shift, from programmatical/transactional thinking, attitudes, and behavior to a culture based on the relationship of one member to another, of member to Temple, of member to Torah and God. Believing in the value and sacredness of relationships, many aspects of life at Temple Shalom continue to be affected. From the first contact of a newcomer to Temple Shalom through the years of being part of our Temple family, the experience of belonging is much more than a financial commitment. Our ultimate goal is to build a community of engaged congregants, a religious home in which the connection between Temple and congregant is centered on our member's needs and what is important to them. Creating the systems that promote relationships and an environment that is conducive to connecting with others are tools for furthering this transformation.

One Family, a three-year-old initiative at Temple Shalom, has engaged in many such systems. Some of the on-going ones are:

- Name badges and cabinet now in our lobby.

- Additional new member engagement opportunities.

- Additional seasonal affiliate opportunities.

- Tribute Garden with seating (see detail below).

- iTemple – a members only, member-driven computer platform connecting our members.

- Live and archived streaming video of services and events in our sanctuary.

- Affinity group for Empty Nesters (more affinity groups to come).

- A "hearing loop" in our sanctuary to assist the participation of congregants with hearing impairment.

- Shabbat Senior Transport – providing rides to and from Erev Shabbat services for those seniors who don't drive.

- Shalom Chaverim – a structure for providing greeters for Erev Shabbat services (to be followed later by providing a similar system for other events held at Temple Shalom) (see detail below).

Our new Tribute Garden was sparked by interest shown at one of the first meetings of our One Family Team. Even though there was no budget with which to complete such a project, the committee was formed and planning began almost immediately. The generosity of several caring members made possible the renovation of the garden space and development of a beautiful garden with trees, shrubs, lawn, and pavers. With the new foliage growing, the second phase has begun. The sale of pavers, benches, plantings, etc. is under way, making this project both a place for quiet contemplation and conversation and a fund raiser for the Temple.

A new system just introduced to the congregation in recent weeks is our Shalom Chaverim project. This group of members, supported by an on-line sign-up system, provides a warm welcome to all who come to our spiritual home for Erev Shabbat services. Shalom Chaverim members assist with name badges, seating, and special needs of those attending services. They keep a watchful eye at the Oneg Shabbat to ensure guests and newcomers are engaged with other attendees.

The support of the Temple Board, our clergy, and our staff have been central to the transformation at Temple Shalom. This support is evidenced by the new mission statement, the new Temple logo, the new member pledge system (L'Shalom), and our Membership and Engagement Coordinator. These changes reflect the values of Relational Judaism, of our One Family. This support is greatly appreciated.

APPENDIX 6E

Web Site Link

2017

The ONE FAMILY INITIATIVE at TEMPLE SHALOM
Naples, Florida

Relational Judaism, implemented as One Family at Temple Shalom, is a way of thinking, a way of doing things. It is who we strive to be. At Temple Shalom, we are in a transformation, a cultural shift, from programmatical/ transactional thinking, attitudes, and behavior to a culture based on the relationship of one member to another, of member to Temple, of member to Torah and God. Believing in the value and sacredness of relationships, many aspects of life at Temple Shalom continue to be affected. From the first contact of a newcomer to Temple Shalom through the years of being part of our Temple family, the experience of belonging is much more than a financial commitment. Our ultimate goal is to build a community of engaged congregants, a religious home in which the connection between Temple and congregant is centered on our member's needs and what is important to them. Creating the systems that promote relationships and an environment that is conducive to connecting with others are tools for furthering this transformation.

✡ ✡ ✡ ✡

Our One Family Initiative is based on the concepts developed by Dr. Ron Wolfson in his book *Relational Judaism: Using the Power of Relationships to Transform the Jewish Community*. One Family is the name by which our Temple Shalom process of transformation is known. Our One Family goals began with . . .

- Increasing connectivity and engagement among our members
- Building and developing relationships for current, new, and potential members
- Creating an intergenerational bridge

These goals do not mandate that our Team develop more programs, rather that we develop systems to assist our members in connecting and engaging and that we create an environment conducive to connectivity and engagement. New programs may well develop, and they have, but the focus of our One Family is creating that cultural shift. To accomplish this change, our One Family Team was formed. With about sixty members on the Team, we meet, brainstorm, consider options, determine next steps, and provide leadership and volunteers to bring our selections to fruition. We worked on these projects in winter, 2014, integrating One Family efforts with existing Temple committees to develop several systems and changes. These initiatives have either been implemented or are in development (more information regarding each can be found at the end of this report):

- Name badges and cabinet now in our lobby.

- Home-based *Shabbat* Dinner structure.

- Additional new member engagement opportunities.

- Additional seasonal affiliate opportunities.

- Many Stories – a structure for one-on-one conversations and story sharing among congregants.

- Redesigned and redecorated Perman Library with conversational seating and coffee bar.

- Tribute Garden with seating (seating coming soon).

- iTemple – a members only, member-driven computer platform connecting our members.

- Techie Tutors – a member helping member technology-learning structure, assisting members with iTemple.

- Live and archived streaming video of services and events in our sanctuary.

- Affinity group for Empty Nesters (more affinity groups to come).

- A "hearing loop" in our sanctuary to assist the participation of congregants with hearing impairment.

- *Shabbat* Senior Transport – providing rides to and from Erev Shabbat services for those seniors who don't drive.

- Hospitality Hosts – A system for welcoming and including members and visitors to our Temple home (being developed, to be implemented soon).

In addition, the increased contact among our members has led to:

- Developing our *Tikkun Olam* Council—a development and coordination body for social action work at Temple Shalom.

- The realization of the need for programming for our senior singles and interfaith families.

✡   ✡   ✡   ✡

To ensure that connections are made and there is follow-through with every effort to connect and engage congregants with each other, with Temple, with our staff, the new position of **Engagement Coordinator and Concierge** has been developed. This staff member is usually the first contact visitors have with the Temple. The Concierge is a friendly and welcoming presence, a provider of that all-important wonderful first impression. The Concierge answers phones and greets people as they enter the building and introduces visitors to other staff members and congregation leaders. In addition, the Concierge follows up on all membership inquiries, helps orient new and potential members with the surrounding community, encourages new and existing members to connect with other congregants, and contacts members on their birthdays and other simchas. By providing consistency in these initial contacts and relationship-building experiences, this staff member makes certain that the connections take place and that the desired connections don't "fall through the cracks." The presence of this Concierge position reflects the importance placed on Relational Judaism, our One Family Initiative, by the Temple Shalom leadership.

Development of Relational Judaism at Temple Shalom, our One Family process of change, is well under way. As we continue this process, we are also promoting the concept of Audacious Hospitality as presented by Rabbi Rick Jacobs, President of The Union for Reform Judaism. The purpose of Audacious Hospitality is "to eliminate the barriers that have prevented people from finding their place in Judaism." It is "about more than being a lovely host. It is being 'an organization that thinks outside the box' in order to allow people to participate and feel they are making a difference." Audacious Hospitality includes much of what we are endeavoring to create . . .

- A warm welcome to our Temple home.

- Reaching beyond active Temple members to less involved members and the unaffiliated, promoting engagement and connection.

- Respect for clergy, staff, and each other.

- Openness to new ideas and doing things in new ways.

Becoming a model of Relational Judaism and an example of Audacious Hospitality is a process, evolving over time, with purpose, with planning, with persistence. It requires support of leadership, involvement of membership, and clarity of vision. As we move forward with this process of cultural change, we welcome the participation of everyone who wants to be (more) involved in this sacred community.

One Family Team

Description of the Systems and Changes
Undertaken by the One Family Initiative

Name Badges – Name badges have been made for every adult member of the congregation including our Seasonal Affiliates. They are housed in a beautiful cabinet in the front lobby of our building. The badges have been well received; our members have become accustomed to wearing them in the building and returning them to the cabinet as they leave. Clip-on or lanyard style name badges are also available for guests.

Shabbat **Dinners** – Those who have hosted or attended home-held Shabbat Dinners have reported very positive experiences. They report meeting new people, developing new relationships, and strengthening existing friendships. A new, visible depiction of these dinners is on display in the hallway across from the Perman Library. These "*Shabbat* Dinner Trains," with host names on the engines and guest names on the cars, provide a visual representation of each dinner. As new dinners are held, new trains will be added. If those who attended a dinner then host a dinner, the connection will be shown. We look forward to watching these Shabbat Dinner Trains grow!

New Member Engagement – This past year, besides the annual New Member Potluck Shabbat Dinner in January, an orientation program was held in December to give our new members an opportunity to meet with our clergy, professional staff, administrative staff, and some of our lay leaders. The program featured a tour of the building including the school areas, office areas, library, chapel, sanctuary, social hall, and kitchen. In addition, our Engagement Coordinator and Concierge, a member of our Temple staff, has been in contact with the new members to help integrate them into the congregation. New members from last fiscal year and this year are also among the congregants being included in this year's one-on-one conversations.

Seasonal Affiliate Engagement – A Seasonal Affiliate Potluck Shabbat Dinner was held in March. Some have suggested that this event be held earlier in the winter season next year to allow the Affiliates to meet one another closer to their arrival in Southwest Florida.

Affinity Groups – One group, the Empty Nesters, has been formed. They have identified likely congregants who might want to participate, held meetings, and discussed program ideas. The Empty Nesters group enjoyed a Passover *seder* and a sunset cruise together in Spring, 2016. Plans are being developed for the 2016-17 year.

Technology Additions –

- **Streaming Video** – The recording of events taking place in the sanctuary was used for the first time for High Holiday services, 2015. The streaming and archiving of services are available through the Temple website and can be viewed by those unable to attend our services. Any event taking place in the sanctuary can be recorded and archived. The recordings can be provided through the website or can be closed and designated for a specific group. The reports from those who have viewed events from the website have been favorable, being very much appreciated by those who were not in town at the time of the event and by those who could not attend due to illness.

- **iTemple** – This internet platform, available only to Temple members, is designed as a member-driven system of connection and communication. Members sharing a similar interest (such as golf, needlework, books, etc.), special interest groups (such as committees, religious school class parents and teachers, Temple Board, etc.) can connect and communicate using this platform. For nearly a year, iTemple has been in use by some Temple groups. After identifying program issues that needed adjustment, iTemple was provided to the entire congregation in February 2016.

- **The Hearing Loop** – This hidden wire loop is used by individuals using hearing aids equipped with a telecoil. Loop technology enhances the experience of individuals with hearing loss by providing sound as it is transmitted from the microphone, eliminating background noise. Sound is amplified using the specifications of the individual's own hearing aid, providing quality sound for the user. In September 2016, and January 2017, orientation programs will be held to demonstrate this technology to those who can benefit from its use.

Techie Tutors – The iTemple platform (above), now available to the whole congregation, provides a great opportunity for members to connect. It is anticipated that many of our members will require assistance in learning to use this platform. The Techie Tutor structure will provide this assistance. Members of the congregation who are users of technology, are being sought to be trained as "tutors" to lead workshops or to work one-on-one with Temple members requesting assistance. The tutors will be trained by our Director of Communication, Jeanette Fischer, and the workshops will be organized through the Techie Tutor structure.

One Family – Many Stories – This initiative formed in spring and summer of 2015, with training workshops for potential volunteer Conversation Leaders. Each Conversation Leader was asked to call four to six members of the congregation and to set up a meeting time and place to engage in one-on-one conversations. These conversations include sharing stories, interests, passions, and ideas for Temple activities. The purpose of these conversations is to create new relationships, strengthen existing relationships among our members, and to identify needed areas of programming. New members beginning July 2015, were among those called. More volunteers are needed to initiate the one-on-one conversations. To date, callers have reported good experiences and have identified programming needs.

Perman Library – This space was reconfigured and redecorated to be, not only the home of our lending library, but the location of the Temple Bean, our coffee station. It is beautifully designed to be connection friendly, with seating conducive to conversation and engagement and small group meetings.

Tribute Garden – The creation of the garden area adjacent to the Social Hall, presented to the congregation Fall, 2015, is a welcome improvement to the front of our building. The garden is expected to be a space for meditation and quiet conversation. Additions to the garden will be benches, plants, and pavered walkways, all of which can be stimulators for fundraising.

***Shabbat* Senior Transport** – A new service beginning September 2016, is transportation for *Erev Shabbat* services to and from Seniors homes for those who do not drive or do not drive at night. This service is available through our Concierge. Reservations can be made by Wednesday, 2 PM; cancellations are requested by noon on Friday.

Hospitality Hosts (referred to as Ambassadors) – A recent addition to the One Family Initiative, still in development, is the plan for welcoming members and visitors to our Temple home for *Shabbat* services and events. Weekly, besides the *Shabbat* Greeters located either outside the front door or inside the lobby as attendees enter, Hospitality Hosts will be placed at locations on the front walk, at the table where visitors name badges are available, at the cabinet where members name badges are kept, and in the sanctuary. They will welcome attendees, assist with name badges, introduce newcomers to other attendees, assist with seating, and locate prayer books as needed. Even though all of our members are encouraged to be inclusive at the *Oneg,* the Hospitality Hosts will be specifically responsible to ensure that no one is alone as we gather and schmooze. The goal is to make certain that everyone who attends services and events at Temple Shalom has a warm welcome, a sense of inclusion, and a "friendly" experience.

If you have questions, want further information, or would like to join in any part of our One Family process, please contact our One Family Chairs.

Handout for Sisterhood & Men's Club Leaders
One Family at Temple Shalom

July 2014

Our Temple Shalom One Family initiative is directed toward relationship development by encouraging our members to connect with one another. Our efforts are channeled through six **Action Groups** in various stages of organizing. The Action Groups and their areas of focus are :

Ambassadors – The focus of this group is to establish a group of volunteers who will welcome visitors, develop processes to integrate new members, dialogue with new, current, and exiting members, and develop avenues that will draw members to participate as members of our Temple family. The existing Membership Committee will be an important part of this Action Group.

***Shabbat* Dinner Action Group** – The focus of this Group is to organize *Shabbat* Dinner and *Havdalah* events of various sizes, configurations, and locations. The events will provide opportunities for our members to share the *Shabbat* or *Havdalah* experience with other members of our Temple family in settings that encourage the development of relationships.

One Family Home Action Group – This Group is focusing on our Temple facility, identifying and exploring ways our building can be more conducive to welcoming visitors to Temple and more conducive to relationship development.

Affinity Groups Action Group – This group is charged with developing various interest groups based on demographic, professional, and other areas of similarity. This effort is being developed using the "empty nesters" as a model affinity group.

Communications/Technology Action Group – This Group is updating the Temple database and developing social medial venues for Temple.

Intergenerational Activities – This Action Group is still in the formation stage. Several people have asked about working with others who wish to develop opportunities for our congregants of varying generations to work together.

Your participation in these or other possible Action Groups is most welcome.

APPENDIX 6G

One-Liners

2016-2017

There were two one-liners in each issue of the monthly bulletin for most of the 2016-2017 year. Each one-liner appeared in a box on different pages of the monthly bulletin. Each one-liner was followed by directions to the Temple website for more information.

August 2016

> **One Family** means members connecting and engaging with each other, with Temple and with Torah.
>
> *For more information, see the Temple Shalom website **www.naplestemple.org** Click on Our Family, then One Family*

> **One Family** means learning each others' "stories."
>
> *For more information, see the Temple Shalom website **www.naplestemple.org** Click on Our Family, then One Family.*

September 2016

One Family is the ability to **CONNECT** even when you can't be at Temple.

One Family is finding others who share your interests.

October 2016

One Family is providing the best possible experience for all who enter our Temple home.

One Family believes in the value and sacredness of relationships.

November 2016

One Family is striving to live our Jewish values.

One Family is encouraging our Temple family to wear their name badges at all services and events.

December 2016

One Family is creating a *Kehilat Kedosha*, a sacred community.

One Family is sharing *Shabbat* Dinners in each other's homes.

January 2017

One Family is a way of thinking, a way of doing things. It is who we strive to be.

One Family is warmly welcoming newcomers into our Family.

March 2017

One Family is including *Mitzvot* in our daily lives, making a difference, repairing the world.

One Family is the experience of belonging and engaging with others, sharing in the life of Temple Shalom.

April 2017

One Family is sharing *Shabbat* Dinners and Services at the beach.

One Family is sharing our skills, talents, and passions to enhance the experience that is Temple Shalom.

APPENDIX 6H

Article in *The Voice*[b] – New Temple Logo

January 2017

A New Logo for Temple Shalom!

Temple ✱ Shalom
One family, many connections

The Marketing and Branding Committee is proud to share the new logo design for Temple Shalom. After several months of meetings and working with a designer, the logo (above) was selected for our use. The logo includes aspects of our ancient heritage as well as our contemporary character.

This logo is inherently and uniquely descriptive of Temple Shalom and representative of our tag line: one family, many connections. We hope you agree with our committee that the new logo is crisp, fresh, and most of all, serves as a meaningful representation of our Temple family.

The graphic display features:

- The Mogen David (Star of David), a central symbol of our Jewish faith.
- The circle of 12 hands reminiscent of the 12 tribes of Israel.
- The circle arrangement of the hands suggestive of our "One Family
- The color variety suggesting our diversity and inclusiveness.
- The connectedness of the hands representing the many connections among our members, working together to create our community.

Thank you to our committee members who worked together in the development of our new logo. Thank you to our Executive Director and our Communications Director for their input.

L'Shalom – First Letter to Members
January 2017

Temple Shalom
One family, many connections

January 24, 2017

L'Shalom: Aligning our Financial Culture with Our Jewish Values

Dear,

As we walk through the doors of Temple Shalom, we are reminded immediately that our Temple is committed to the values of One Family: relationships, engagement and inclusion. When we give financial support to the Temple, our mode of giving should reflect those values. The concept of billed dues is an imperfect fit with these core values.

That's why the leadership of Temple Shalom has initiated a new approach for raising the necessary funds to sustain our Temple, replacing our former monetary support structure. Starting July 1, 2017, we are asking you to support Temple Shalom by offering an annual pledge, which we call L'Shalom ("For Temple Shalom").

L'Shalom, our new pledge system, is based on our ancient Jewish tradition. In the Book of Exodus we read how our Israelite ancestors brought gifts as their hearts moved them to finance the construction of the Mishkan, the Tabernacle. L'Shalom continues our tradition of accepting what is offered willingly to sustain our sacred space.

How will this work?

L'Shalom is based on the generosity of our congregants. We will ask each household to pledge an annual financial commitment to the Temple. As a guide for your support, we will provide the sustaining amount, based upon our current budgetary needs. We ask all households that are able, to pledge this sustaining amount. We know that many will continue their current generosity by pledging more. At the same time, those who are not able to give at this sustaining level may pledge as they are able. We ask you to do the best you can. By asking you to determine your own pledges, we are removing barriers to membership and participation. Religious School fees, Above and Beyond, and fundraising will continue, separate from L'Shalom. Every pledge, no matter the size, will be valued and honored. As always, the confidentiality of your commitment will be respected.

Are we crazy?

We don't think so! Is this fundamental change risk free? Certainly not! But we strongly believe that this innovative approach is in keeping with our commitment to maintaining Temple Shalom as a place for meaningful relationships and life- long engagement. We value all that the Temple offers to our families and community and want it to remain an open, welcoming spiritual center and place of learning. Together, we will ensure Temple Shalom's well-being long into the future.

We have planned open forums at the Temple to discuss what this change means and how it will be implemented on the following dates:

Sunday, February 5, 2017 at 9:15 a.m.
Wednesday, February 8, 2017 at 2:00 p.m.
Thursday, February 16, 2017 at 10:00 a.m.
Tuesday, February 21, 2017 at 7:30 p.m.

Refreshments will be served at each meeting; R.S.V.P.'s are recommended.

More information about L'Shalom is available on our website. This information will be mailed to you, together with a request for your pledge for our next fiscal year, at the end of February.

If you have questions or wish to comment, please feel free to contact our Executive Director or our Membership and Engagement Coordinator.

L'Shalom

President   Rabbi   Cantor

APPENDIX 6J

Temple Shalom Website – *L'Shalom* FAQs

January 2017 – Present

L'SHALOM—FREQUENTLY ASKED QUESTIONS

> *Everyone whose heart stirred him and everyone whose spirit moved him came and brought the portion of the Lord's contribution for the work of the Tent of Meeting.*
>
> *(Exodus 35:21)*

Why are we changing to a pledge system? We are deeply committed to the Temple being accessible to everyone, regardless of financial circumstances. We treasure your partnership in our community and want our commitment process to reflect our values. We are aligning our financial practices with our values.

What is a pledge system? Rather than being assessed dues, members of the congregation will determine and pledge their annual financial contribution, their *L'Shalom* commitment.

Is this system different from the old system? Yes. L'Shalom differs from our previous annual commitment model in three important ways. First, while we recommend a sustaining amount to pledge, the actual L'Shalom commitment is up to each member. There will be no specified amount required to be a part of our Temple family. Second, no one must request an adjustment to their financial obligation to Temple, because they themselves will determine that obligation. Third, with L'Shalom, we eliminate the separate categories of membership or affiliation previously in place. We will all be members of Temple Shalom, entitled to vote, attend High Holy Day services, and participate equally.

When will the new *L'Shalom* system be implemented? On July 1, 2017, the beginning of Fiscal Year 2017-2018.

How will pledging work? In February, Temple will send out pledge forms, and announce the "sustaining amount," the amount we are asking all adult members to pledge for the coming fiscal year. Please complete and return the pledge form to Temple by (DATE). **If you submit no pledge form by (DATE), Temple will assume you plan to pay the sustaining amount.** At the end of June, you will receive a statement for next year which reflects the amount you pledged, or the default sustaining amount if you have not sent in a pledge.

Does *L'Shalom* change my current year's annual commitment to Temple Shalom? No. Your annual commitment for our current fiscal year (July 1, 2016 – June 30, 2017) remains the same as it was.

What does the pledge cover? Does it cover school fees? Your pledge, regardless of amount, gives you full membership in the Temple for all family members living in your household. Other fees, such as Religious School tuition, Bar/Bat Mitzvah fees, and Pre-school fees will be assessed separately.

How do I know how much to pledge? What if I cannot give the sustaining amount? We hope that all those who are able will pledge the sustaining amount or more. If you do not pledge the sustaining amount, please make a financial commitment to Temple Shalom appropriate for you in light of your circumstances, and which recognizes and honors our responsibilities to each other, to our Temple Community, and to our Jewish future.

Will there be categories of pledge commitment similar to Above and Beyond? No. *L'Shalom* will reflect our belief that every member is an equal partner in our One Family. So there will be no "categories" of pledges.

Will my pledge be confidential? As with dues in past years, your pledge will be confidential. Only those involved directly with maintaining Temple's financial records (our bookkeeper, executive director, and our treasurer) have routine access to individual members' giving information.

Does my pledge remain the same from year to year? That is up to you. You will be asked to fill out a new pledge form each year.

How is the sustaining amount calculated? The sustaining amount is calculated each year by taking the total of Temple's anticipated expenses for the next fiscal year, deducting all anticipated income to be raised aside from *L'Shalom*, and then dividing that number by the approximate number of adult members of Temple Shalom.

Will fundraising, such as Above and Beyond, continue? Yes. Fundraising will continue to be necessary to ensure Temple Shalom's financial viability.

What happens if I have a balance to my Building Fund commitment? The sustaining amount includes ongoing costs for maintaining our facility. Therefore, Building Fund commitments scheduled to be billed after June 30, 2017 will be released.

I live here for only a portion of the year, and am an Associate or Affiliate Member. What should I pledge? Your *L'Shalom* pledge should reflect that you are a part of our One Family, and share in the benefits and obligations of being a Temple member while you are here, in a manner financially reasonable for you. Pledging an amount equal to your previous annual commitment would be an appropriate guideline. If you can pledge more, it would be greatly appreciated.

What should I pledge if I have a Young Family or Young Single Membership? There are many factors which fairly affect how much each individual can and should pledge. We simply ask that you look into your heart and make a pledge of support for the entire congregation, given your particular circumstances. Pledging an amount equal to your previous annual commitment would be an appropriate guideline. If you can pledge more, it would be greatly appreciated.

What happens to previous unpaid balances? If you have any pre-existing financial obligations to the Temple when you receive your statement, please contact our Executive Director to discuss.

As did our Biblical forebears,
let "our hearts be stirred and our spirits moved" in our pledges to L'Shalom.

APPENDIX 6K

L'Shalom – Second Letter to Members and Pledge Card

March 2017

One family, many connections

March 20, 2017

Dear   ,

As we first shared in January, we are replacing the traditional dues structure at Temple Shalom with *L'Shalom*, a voluntary pledge system.

In the Book of Exodus we read that Moses asked the people of Israel to bring gifts as their hearts moved them to build the *Mishkan*, the portable sanctuary in the midst of the desert. Moses was overwhelmed by their generosity as the Israelites invested in their future. We modeled *L'Shalom* on this concept of making gifts from the heart, asking members to give meaningfully. Our expectation is that our new *L'Shalom* pledge system will build on our members' past generosity as we generate the funds necessary to sustain our temple.

The sustaining level of giving for 2017-2018 is $ per single adult household. The sustaining level is the amount that is required for us to maintain our exemplary programming, remarkable clergy and staff, and provide for the operations of our congregation. It also includes the cost of providing additional security for the temple, a vital necessity in today's world. The sustaining amount was carefully considered by the temple finance committee and reviewed by the Temple Shalom Board of Trustees.

Your commitment for this current year was $. You are a vital part of our Temple Shalom family, and therefore we ask that your pledge reflects what your heart feels and what you can afford. Any amount that you pledge over the sustaining level will be recognized as a contribution to *Above and Beyond*. We are eager for you to continue your relationship with Temple Shalom —not just as a member, but as an active partner.

Enclosed are your *L'Shalom* pledge form and a reply envelope as well as responses to a list of frequently asked questions about *L'Shalom*. Please review the enclosed materials. If you have questions or need further clarification, contact the temple office.

We ask that you return your pledge form by Friday, April 21, so that we can use the information to assist with budgeting for 2017-2018.

We look forward to having you as part of our Temple Shalom Family for years to come.

B'Shalom

Temple Shalom
One family, many connections

Your commitment for 2016-2017 was

☐ I am pleased to make a *L'Shalom* pledge for July, 2017 to June, 2018 at the
Sustaining Level of $ (for single adult household).
Amounts pledged over the sustaining amount will be considered as part of your *Above and Beyond* gift.

☐ I am pleased to make a *L'Shalom* pledge for July, 2017 to June, 2018
for $_____.

Your *L'Shalom* pledge is greatly appreciated.

_____ _____
                     Signature   *Date*

Please return your signed pledge card in the envelope provided by Friday, April 21, 2017

APPENDIX 6L

Article in *The Shabbat Shalom*[a] –
Reminder to Members to Return Pledge Cards

March 2017

Temple Shalom

One family, many connections

L'Shalom

reminder!

We want to hear from you.....

If you have not yet returned your *L'Shalom* pledge, please be sure to return the enclosed card no later than May 15th.

We truly need to hear from all our members in order to be able to make plans for our next fiscal year. Please know that, as stated in our questions and answers, if we do not receive your pledge form we will assume you are pledging the sustaining amount.

If you have any questions about the *L'Shalom* program or your pledge, please contact the Temple office.

APPENDIX 6M

L'Shalom – Second Year Letter to Congregation and Pledge Card

April 2018

Temple ✡ Shalom

One family, many connections

April 2018

«FamilyID»

Dear,

This past year we embarked on a new journey of aligning Temple Shalom's financial needs with Jewish values by replacing our traditional dues structure with L'Shalom, a voluntary pledge system.

The L'Shalom model draws inspiration from Torah, where we read that Moses asked the people of Israel to bring gifts as their hearts moved them to build the Mishkan, the mobile worship center. Moses was overwhelmed by their generosity. We, too, are in awe of your response to this new approach. In the past year our membership has grown by more than 100 households! We met our goals for the funds necessary to sustain our congregation, fulfill the needs of members and further enhance the relational nature of our One Family. In addition, we were able to be a resource for our community during and after Hurricane Irma.

Encouraged by these results, we are moving forward into the second year of L'Shalom. We are pleased to maintain the same sustaining level as last year. For 2018-2019, the amount we recommend each household pledge so that we meet the Temple budget is $ per household (or $ for a household with one adult). This amount was carefully determined by the Temple finance committee, and then reviewed by the Temple Board of Trustees. Included in this calculation are the costs for serving the needs of our growing congregation, as well as increased security measures for the safety of our Temple Family.

Your 2017-2018 L'Shalom pledge amount was $«Total_2018_Pledged_amount». As a vital part of our Temple Shalom family, we ask that your pledge reflects what your heart feels and what you can afford. (Like last year, any amount that you pledge above the sustaining amount will be recognized as a contribution to Above & Beyond.)

Enclosed are your L'Shalom pledge form and a reply envelope. Please review the enclosed materials. If you have questions or need further clarification, contact our Membership Engagement Coordinator and Concierge. We ask that you return your pledge form by Friday, May 21, so that we can use the information to assist with our financial planning for 2018-2019. If we do not hear from you by May 21 we will assume that you are making your pledge at the sustaining level.

We look forward to your active engagement in Temple Shalom's One Family for years to come.

L'Shalom

President   Rabbi   Cantor

Temple Shalom

One family, many connections

I/We are pleased to make a *L'Shalom* pledge for 2018-2019 at the sustaining level of $ _____ (two or more adult household).

I am pleased to make a *L'Shalom* pledge for 2018-2019 at the sustaining level of $ _____ (single adult household).

I/We are pleased to make a L'Shalom pledge for 2018-2019 in the amount of $_____.

Amounts pledged above the sustaining amount will be considered as part of your Above & Beyond pledge.

Your *L'Shalom* pledge is greatly appreciated.

_____   _____
Signature(s)   Date

Please return your signed pledge card in the envelope provided by Monday, May 21, 2018.
If we do not hear from you by May 21 we will assume that you are making your pledge at the sustaining level.

Havurah Invitation, Cover Letter & Application

Would you like to join a Havurah?

The word *havurah*—חֲבוּרָה comes from the Hebrew word *haver*—חָבֵר meaning friend.

A *havurah* is a Jewish group, especially an informal one, that meets regularly.

Temple Shalom
One family, many connections

Why join a *Havurah*?

Being part of a *havurah* provides members of Temple Shalom with an opportunity to develop and strengthen friendships with others who share similar interests. Whether you're a new member looking to meet other congregants or an existing member seeking new friendships, a *havurah* is a great way to create an extended family within the Temple Shalom community.

Each *havurah* is a small community of congregants who gather together to socialize, learn more about Jewish subjects, celebrate Jewish holidays, or explore any focus that the group chooses. The group is encouraged to create programs that celebrate Jewish life and build community. A *havurah* may consist of singles, couples, families or any combination of the above. Typically, a *havurah* has at most 20 members or 8-10 families.

Each *havurah* defines its own goals and means for growth and self-expression. Some *havurot* (pl.) will meet many times throughout the year, such as monthly, while others will meet less frequently. The *havurah* may meet in a member's home or at a destination such as a restaurant, park, museum or theater.

Typical activities may include:

- Creating holiday celebrations
- Joining together for Shabbat meals
- Working on a volunteer project
- Attending Temple activities together or meeting afterwards
- Arranging a group outing to a local museum, park, concert, etc.

To learn more about joining a havurah, contact:

Temple Shalom
One family, many connections

Please indicate your interest in joining a havurah by completing the form below.
We look forward to connecting you with other members at Temple Shalom.

Name(s):			Date:	
Current address:				
City:		State:	Zip Code:	
Phone Number:		Additional Phone #:		
Mobile Number:		Additional Mobile #:		
Email:		Additional email:		

Age Range: ☐20-29 ☐30-39 ☐40-49 ☐50-59 ☐60-69 ☐70-79 ☐80+

Retired: ☐ Yes ☐ No ☐ Full Time Resident ☐ Seasonal Resident

CHILDREN AT HOME:

Name	Age

HOW WOULD YOU DESCRIBE YOURSELF?

☐ Senior ☐ Interfaith Family ☐ Empty Nester ☐ Single ☐ Family with young children
☐ Foodie ☐ Family with teenagers ☐ Working family ☐ Other_____

INTERESTS

☐ Social ☐ Jewish Study ☐ Sports ☐ Social Action ☐ The Arts ☐ Holiday Celebrations
☐ Outdoors ☐ Family Activities ☐ Outdoors ☐ Other_____

COMMENTS

Please return this page to:
Temple Shalom
Membership and Engagement Coordinator

Havurah Handbook

Front Cover

Temple **&** Shalom

One family, many connections

HAVURAH

HANDBOOK

Havurah Handbook

Table of Contents

Table of Contents

Havurah Handbook

Page One

What is a Havurah?

A *havurah* is a group of 5-8 families or up to 20 individuals who get together on a regular basis to celebrate Jewish life. The difference between a *havurah* and any other social group is that all members must make a commitment to the group to meet regularly once a month.

What's the advantage of a Havurah?

Getting to know people in a larger congregation can be intimidating. A *havurah* is a terrific way to become acquainted with others who live near you, and have similar interests.

What kinds of activities does a Havurah do?

It's up to you! Your group can enjoy a Shabbat dinner together, have a Chanukah party, build a Sukkah, and even go camping if you're so inclined. Each *havurah* determines the types of activities it wants to do. Temple Shalom's Membership Engagement Coordinator, is available to help with programming ideas if needed.

How do you get a Havurah together?

After returning a completed *havurah* application, you will be "matched up" with others who have similar preferences.

Membership Policy and Procedures

1. Using group consensus as a model, towards the beginning of your *havurah's* inception, discuss your group's optimal membership size. - Establish your group's minimum and maximum size (in either number of families or number of people).

2. All *havurah* members must be members of Temple Shalom- If you do not have specific congregants in mind, consider the characteristics that you are looking for:

   - Number of members
   - Ages range
   - Checklist of basic interests you'd like them to have in common
   - Regularly scheduled meeting dates and times

1 | Page

Havurah Handbook

Page Two

Call the Membership Engagement Coordinator at Temple Shalom if you need assistance selecting additional participants.

3. Once a *havurah* invites an applicant to one of it's meetings, the applicant is considered a member of that group, if the applicant so chooses. Welcome and include new members. Invite them to participate in the decision making and responsibilities of the *havurah*.

4. Inform the Temple Shalom Membership Engagement Coordinator of any changes in membership in order to keep our mailing lists accurate.

"How-To" Guide for New and Ongoing Havurot

1. Program Planning Meeting
   a. Decide frequency of meetings. Ideally, once a month.
   b. Brainstorm possible programs. Reach a consensus of ideas and activities that will satisfy the majority of your membership.
   c. Consider including a combination of social, educational, cultural and religious events throughout. You may also wish to include discussions of Jewish issues, inviting a guest speaker from the synagogue or community, or attending a specific Temple Shalom function or service.
   d. REMIND each member in advance to bring his/her personal calendar to this planning meeting.
   e. Divide up the responsibilities for the program planning meeting: secretary, phone calls, refreshments, etc.
   f. Decide on a specific time for monthly meetings (Ex: every third Sunday of the month). Plan a monthly schedule of meetings with dates, locations and program ideas in advance for at least the next six months.
   g. Decide who wants to take responsibility for each aspect of the programs. This can be done at random, alphabetically by last name, or simply those who are

2 | Page

Havurah Handbook

Page Three

interested can take responsibility for aspects of a specific program.

   i. If the host family of a certain program is unable to hold its assigned meeting or program, assign another family to substitute. If this is not feasible, then the yearly schedule should continue as planned and the original host family will miss their turn and await the next rotation of assignments.

   h. Send out a copy of the finalized schedule of programs to each member. Include a roster of membership with names, addresses, phone numbers and email. You may also wish to include a list of birthdays, wedding anniversaries, etc.

2. Handling Finances

   a. Some havurot collect monthly dues that can be put towards speakers, special presents, donations to honor a member, charitable functions, or to save towards a Havurah program. This is not required and should be discussed among members.

How To Successfully Chair Your Assigned Havurah Meeting

1. Each *havurah* member/family should get a copy of the calendar for the year that includes days of meetings and activities. This will clarify specific program assignments and allow members to schedule accordingly.

2. Send a reminder email to members of your *havurah* 10 days prior to a program requesting some form of RSVP and include travel directions to the meeting location.

3. When you are in charge of a program prepare early and plan ahead. Consider sending relevant reading materials to the members of your *havurah* at least 10 days ahead of time. Prepare in advance some key questions or information to help start the discussion, if needed.

4. Encourage *havurah* members to arrive on time and begin your meeting promptly. The person or couple responsible for the program might choose to conduct the meeting or

3 | Page

Havurah Handbook

Page Four

program. If a guest speaker is involved, you might wish to call him/her a week prior to make sure time and travel directions are clear, and to inquire if he/she will require any assistance.

5. Plan ahead! Coordinate refreshments in advance. Determine who will bring/provide them, how and when they will be served. Consider these possibilities for handling refreshments:

    a. Members chairing program in their home provide refreshments.

    b. When you have program responsibility, hold the program in another members home with them handling refreshments

    c. Preparation of any food to be shared by all members in a potluck

6. Try to conduct the program in an organized manner. You might consider this simple agenda:

    a. Welcome/Call meeting to order

    b. Discuss old and new business

    c. Announcements

    d. Presentation of preplanned program with discussion

    e. Social time and refreshments

7. Remind your *havurah* of upcoming events of interest at Temple Shalom and in the Naples community. Some events may prove to be a great activity for the entire *havurah* to attend together. Perhaps one member of the *havurah* can volunteer to research this information each 6 months-year and the group as a whole can integrate these events into future calendars.

8. When planning your assigned program, consider asking others to help you. Utilize any resources available to you and don't hesitate to delegate responsibilities if it will make the program more interesting or easier for you. Draw from your own inner desires to strengthen your Jewish ties. You will then enrich yourself and every member of your *havurah*.

4 | Page

Havurah Handbook

Page Five

Discussion Triggers

Havurot are often frustrated by the futility of small talk. In an effort to get people to reveal more of themselves, and to encourage discussion of personal values and experience, try asking open ended questions or using the following prompts:

- Most significant book, poem, play or person...

- Most memorable Jewish moment...

- A good Jew is one who...

- I hope my children remember me as...

- The Jewish Community's most pressing problem is...

- My first Jewish memory is...

- If I won a million dollars in the lottery I would..

Havurah Handbook

Page Six

What's Your Name?

Each *havurah* has a special identity. At your first meeting, as you discuss your goals for the group, it can be a lot of fun to decide on a name that reflects some aspect of your group's personality. It also is a lot easier to refer to the group by name in any correspondence from the synagogue or in an article for Temple Shalom's newsletter or web site.

The following are a few suggestions for names. They can be Hebrew, English, fun, serious, or whatever you might like. Feel free to choose one of these, or make up your own.

Please check with the Membership Engagement Coordinator to make sure your name has not already been chosen.

Aba and Ima(Father and Mother)

Shpielers Tikkun (Spiritual work)

Havanah (Understanding)

Chug (Circle) the world)

Achdut (Unity) *Emet* (Truth)

Jerusalem (or any city in Israel)

Tzadikim (Righteous)

Achei Nefesh (Soul Brothers)

Etz Chaim (Tree of Life)

Kesher (Communication)

Tzibur (Community)

Achvah (Fraternity)

Fressers (Yiddish for "love to eat)

Kevutzah (Group)

Yachad (United)

Ahavah (Love)

Garin (Nucleus)

Kinnus (Gathering)

Yom Rishon (Sunday, 'first day')

Ahieezim (Funny Ones)

Gesher (Bridge)

L'Chaim (To Life)

Zahav (Gold)

Aleph (or any other Hebrew letter)

G'ulim (The Redeemers)

Limud (Study)

Hatikvah (Hope)

Anachnu (We)

Hava Nagila ("Let's be Joyful")

Maa gal (Circle)

Barak (Lightning)

Maven (Expert)

Bent Yeclidut (Friendly Alliance)

Shalom (Peace)

Chai *(Life)*

Shemesh (Sun)

Chatzu teem (From Chutzpah)

Shevet (Tribe)

Chaverim (Friends)

Shira (Song or Poetry)

Chayim (Life)

Shomnim (The Watchmen)

ONE CONGREGATION'S JOURNEY OF CHANGE

Havurah Handbook

Page Seven

Sample Havurah Calendar

January: Volunteer to prepare and serve food at a local homeless shelter

February: Organizational meeting and potluck dinner or a tree planting program for Tu B'Shevat

March: Attend the Temple Shalom's Purim carnival together or make baskets of hamantashen and sweets to take to a retirement home and distribute to senior citizens.

April: Attend a Passover Seder

May: Saturday night potluck dinner

June: Shabbat on the beach

July: Night out to enjoy a movie or concert

August: Havurah weekend away

September: Organizational meeting and potluck dinner or breakfast after Yom Kippur

October: Build a Sukkah and have a Sukkot party

November: Attend Shabbat dinner at Temple Shalom

December: Hanukkah party with candles, food, games and small gifts.

Reminder: Hosts of scheduled events should notify Havurah members of event details (preferably in writing) at least 10 days before the scheduled event.

Havurah Handbook

Page Eight

Sample Planning Questionnaire

(Send in advance of the Program Planning Meeting)

To help our planning meetings proceed and ensure that our havurah is doing what you want please read, fill out, and bring the following information to our next planning meeting.

Please consider the direction that you would like the havurah to take. We will discuss your ideas at our upcoming meeting. This is your/our group and it is important to be sure that the activities reflect the interests and values of all participants.

Please list which month you would like to sponsor an event

First Choice: _____ Second Choice: _____

Please list two or more activities you would like the *havurah* to be involved in for the coming year:

1._____

2._____

Should we expand on topics that have been brought up in the past for discussion?   ☐Yes ☐ No

If yes, please indicate which ones:

_____
_____
_____

Do we have a good balance of educational and social meetings?
                                                                                  ☐Yes ☐No

If no, please give a brief explanation:

_____
_____
_____

Please elaborate on any additional thoughts or ideas

_____
_____
_____
_____

8 | Page

Havurah Handbook

Page Nine

Top 10 Favorite Havurah Tips

1. Decide what you want to do, and what your general goals are based on a combination of social activities, Jewish issues, holiday celebrations, etc.

2. Try and reach a consensus which satisfies the majority of people. This might require patience and some "give and take".

3. Plan a monthly schedule with dates, locations, and programs at least six months in advance.

4. Send out a copy of the entire schedule to each member, and then send out monthly meeting reminders 10 days to two weeks before each meeting with RSVP notices.

5. Fulfill your commitment to each other by doing your share.

6. Attend regularly and make your havurah a priority. Work together to make the meeting something you look forward to.

7. Talk things over if there are conflicts, but be sensitive to the feelings of others.

8. Recognize the dynamics of your own havurah, and based on those dynamics, be realistic about what you do. Some groups will become real extended families; others will develop some close friendships within the group and many will enjoy a variety of experiences together. Others will be united in their dedication to Judaic study. Don't compare yourselves but strive for the elements that make your havurah special to you.,.with the following exception: Everyone in each havurah should share a common desire to strengthen your Jewish ties, to enrich yourself Jewishly, to reach out to other synagogue members, and to have fun!

9. Remind your havurah of coming events of interest at the synagogue and in the Jewish community. Check The Voice and the Federation Star for details. Some of the events may prove to be great activities for the entire havurah to attend together. (Perhaps one member of the havurah may choose to research this information on a monthly basis.)

10. Appoint a havurah liaison as a way of keeping in touch with Temple Shalom and other chavurot.

Havurah Handbook

Page Eleven

Library Resources

The following books might be helpful or interesting guides.

- *The Havurah, A Contemporary Jewish Experience,* Bernard Reisman
- *The Jewish Experiential Book,* Bernard Reisman
- *The First Jewish Catalogue: A Do-it-yourself Kit,* by Siegel and Strassfeld
- *The Second Jewish Catalogue: A Do-it yourself Kit,* by Siegel and Strassfeld
- *The Third Jewish Catalogue: A Do-it-yourself Kit,* by Siegel and Strassfeld (includes a cumulative index)
- *The Jewish Family Book,* Sharon Strassfeld
- *Jewish Values and Social Crisis,* Albert Vorspan
- *The Jewish Encyclopedia Life Is With People,* M. Zborowski
- *The Jewish Directory and Almanac,* Ivan L. Tillem, cci.
- *Explaining Christmas to the Jewish Child,* Lois Miller Weinstein
- *The Shabbat Catalog,* Ruth Brin
- *The Jewish People's Almanac,* David Gross
- *When Bad Things Happen to Good People,* Rabbi Harold Kushner
- *God Wrestling,* Arthur Waskow
- *The Jewish Trivia and Information Book Trivia Judaica,* Ian Shapoisky
- *Generation Without Memory,* Anne Roiphe
- *An Orphan in History,* Paul Cowan
- *A Certain People; American Jews and Their Lives Today,* Charles E. Silberman
- *Back to the Sources; Reading the Classic Jewish Texts,* Barry W. Holtz, ed.
- *Basic Jewish Philosophy*
  - *The Nine Questions People Ask About Judaism,* Prager & Telushkin
  - *Basic Judaism,* Steinberg
  - *What is a Jew?,* Rabbi Morris Kertzer. A guide to beliefs, traditions and practices of

---

Havurah Handbook
Page Twelve

- Judaism
    - Pirke Avot: Sayings of the Fathers, Hertz
    - Philosophies of Judaism, Guttman
    - The Story of Jewish Philosophy, Blau
- Jewish Practices
    - Festivals of Jews, Schauss
    - The Jewish Home Advisor, Kolatch
- Jewish History
    - Jews, God and History, Dimant
    - Wanderings, Potok
    - My People: The Story of the Jews, Eban
    - Any book by Grayzel, Sachar, Roth or Bamberger Holocaust
    - The Abandonment of the Jews, Wyman
    - The War Against the Jews, Dawidowiez
    - Rise and Fall of the Third Reich, Shirer Mysticism
    - Major Trends in Jewish Mysticism, Scholem Immigrant History
    - World of our Fathers, Howe
    - Our Crowd, Birmingham
- Israel
    - The Israelis, Elon (950.01)
    - OJerusalem, LaPierre and Collins (950.11)
    - Arab and Jew: Wounded Spirits in a Promised Land, Shipler (953,23)
- Yiddish
    - The Joys of Yiddish, Rosten
- Biography
    - The Labyrinth of Exile: A Life of Theodor Herzl, B.H. Pawel
    - Begin: The Haunted Spirit
    - Einstein: The Life and Times
    - Freud: A Life for our Times, Gay

APPENDIX 8C
Havurot Meeting Agenda

AGENDA

How to Havurah Meeting

Date | time **Thursday, April 26, 2018 | 7:00pm-8:00pm |**

Agenda Items

- ❖ Welcome

- ❖ Introductions

- ❖ History of Havurah at Temple Shalom

- ❖ Member Introductions

  - ➤ Name

  - ➤ Where are you from?

  - ➤ How long have you been a member?

  - ➤ Why did you want to join a Havurah?

  - ➤ Name 3 favorite activities/pastimes

- ❖ Group Activity

- ❖ Havurah Group Information Worksheet

- ❖ Closing Remarks

GLOSSARY OF HEBREW TERMS USED IN THIS BOOK

Bar/Bat Mitzvah – Rite of passage for boys/girls at the age of thirteen which marks formal entry as responsible adult members of the community

Beresheit – The Hebrew title of the first book of Torah. Usually translated as, "In the beginning . . ."

Bimah – The raised platform at the front of the sanctuary where the service is lead

D'var Torah – A teaching or small sermon; the phrase literally means, "A word of Torah"; little Torah lesson

Erev Shabbat – The evening when Sabbath begins; Friday evening

Good Shabbos – Good Sabbath; a Sabbath greeting

Havdalah – Ceremony at the end of the Sabbath separating the Sabbath from other days of the week, and starting the new week

Havurah (Havurot, pl.) – a group (groups) of friends; an established group of Temple members

Kiddush – Blessing recited to sanctify a holy time, usually performed over wine or grape juice

Kishke Level – Gut level

Mishkan – literally, tent; often refers to a mobile worship structure built and used by the Israelites during their Exodus from Egypt; place of worship

Mi Shebeirach – Literally – "May the One Who Blessed." Commonly used as short-hand for a healing prayer that begins with the formula *"Mi Shebeirach Avoteinu v'Imoteinu* – May the One who blessed our fathers and mothers . . . " Also called *"Mi Shebeirach for Healing."*

Mitzvah (Mitzvot, pl.) – Commandment (Commandments); commonly used to refer to a good deed. The Jewish sages teach that there are 613 positive and negative commandments.

Motzi – Term used to refer to the blessing recited before one eats bread or grain products which ends with, *"Ha-Motzi Lechem Min Ha-Aretz* – The One Who brings forth bread from the earth."* Frequently recited at the start of any meal where one eats bread.

Oneg Shabbat – Social gathering after the Erev Shabbat service

Pirke Avot – "Sayings of the Fathers"; a Jewish text that teaches Jewish ethics by sharing numerous brief and quotable statements; written as part of the Mishnah, a legal text from the 2nd century CE (over 50 generations old) in brief quotable statements

Shabbat – Also known as the Sabbath, the seventh day of the week; designated as a day of rest on which one refrains from work in accordance with the rhythm of the Creation story in which God worked for six days to create the world and rested on the seventh day; begins on Friday at sundown and concludes Saturday at sundown

Shabbat Shalom – "May you have a peaceful Shabbat"; Sabbath peace; a Sabbath greeting

Shalom Chaverim – "Welcome friends"; at Temple Shalom, a group of Sabbath greeters; title of a well-known children's song

Seder – literally, order; the ceremonial Passover dinner

Sukkah – A small hut with a roof open to the stars used during the harvest holiday of Sukkot

Tikkun Olam – "Repair of the world"; often used referring to social action/social justice activities

TANAKH – The three parts of the Hebrew Bible which can be divided into three distinct sections: Torah (the Pentateuch), The Prophets, The Writings; the term Tanakh is an acronym made up of the Hebrew names for the three sections (Torah, Nivi'im, and Ketuvim)

Torah – The Pentateuch; the Five Books of Moses

www.ingramcontent.com/pod-product-compliance
Lightning Source LLC
Chambersburg PA
CBHW080700110426

42739CB00034B/3344